Writing Science Fiction
and Fantasy

Crawford Kilian

Self-Counsel Press
(a division of)
International Self-Counsel Press Ltd.
USA   Canada

Self-Counsel Press acknowledges the financial support of the Government of Canada through the Book Publishing Industry Development Program (BPIDP) for our publishing activities.

Printed in Canada.

First edition: 1998; Reprinted: 1999
Second edition: 2007

Library and Archives Canada Cataloguing in Publication

Kilian, Crawford, 1941–

   Writing science fiction and fantasy / Crawford Kilian. — 2nd ed.

(Self-counsel writing series)
Accompanied by a CD-ROM.
ISBN 978-1-55180-785-0

   1. Science fiction — Authorship. 2. Fantastic fiction — Authorship.
I. Title. II. Series.

PN3377.5.S3K54 2007   808.3'876   C2007-901133-0

Self-Counsel Press
(a division of)
International Self-Counsel Press Ltd.

1704 North State Street   1481 Charlotte Road
Bellingham, WA 98225   North Vancouver, BC V7J 1H1
USA   Canada

Contents

Preface

In the decade since the first edition of this book appeared, the basics of storytelling haven't changed, but resources for storytellers have expanded enormously. The World Wide Web, which no writer foresaw except Mark Twain, has made it easy to do research, seek encouragement, find readers, find publishers, and even become your own publisher.

So for this second edition I've used the web extensively to enhance the content of the print on paper. The CD that comes with the book offers a number of resources. Every topic, author, and book I mention has at least one link on the CD that will take you to more information, and in some cases, to the entire text of the work I refer to, available to read online.

You'll also find links to sites where you can research potential agents, learn what particular publishers require in their submissions, and get a sense of what to expect in a contract.

The CD also contains several of my magazine articles and book reviews, dealing with topics ranging from 19th-century classic SF and particular writing techniques, to how the Internet has affected the writer-reader relationship, particularly in the SF community. Apologies to Mac users — the CD materials are designed for PCs only. However, I have posted these items on my blog Writing Fiction (http://crofsblogs.typepad.com/fiction/) as PDFs.

As for the book itself, much of the material has been reorganized and updated. I have also added an appendix: the annotated first chapter of my work in progress, *Henderson's Tenants*. It's an attempt to show how I try to follow my own advice, and I hope you find it useful.

I wish you every success in all your writing projects.

Introduction

THE CHALLENGE OF WRITING SCIENCE FICTION AND FANTASY

Embarking on a writing career is a real challenge, and the tests are as frightening as anything faced by your favorite literary characters. If you urgently need to define your identity as "writer," you risk failure at every step. Maybe you have a hard time telling a story. Or you can tell it but can't finish it. Maybe you can finish it but can't quit polishing it. Or you can't tell it well enough to get it published. It probably won't be a bestseller, never mind a classic that will survive you and inspire future readers to take up writing. The higher your ambitions, the farther you risk falling.

Like your characters, you're on a quest. The word "quest" comes from the Latin *quaestio* — which means both a seeking and an asking. You are seeking a career as a writer, and asking whether you have the capability for it. You may not always find what you seek or get the answers you want. You know that not every quest ends in glory. But if you really have the writer's vocation, you're already on your way.

One of the archetypal characters in any quest is the clever slave or dwarf who carries a bag of "needments." Every time the hero gets in a jam, the dwarf whips something useful out of the bag and the quest goes on. This book may help provide your needments if you're interested in writing science fiction or fantasy.

But don't consider the advice I offer as the last word or the only word. Science fiction and fantasy can be, and should be, highly individual expressions of universal experience. My expression will not be yours. I have strong opinions about what makes good or bad SF, spellbinding fantasy, or plain old misspelled garbage. Your opinions will surely differ from mine. But if rejecting my views at least helps you articulate your own more clearly, then this book is doing its job.

Here's the job I hope it does: First, it shows you how to save time, energy, and grief by mastering the craft of storytelling as quickly as possible. Second, it suggests how to market your story as quickly as possible. And finally, it tries to persuade you to go beyond the market. If all you do is try to write for the existing market, you are betraying your craft, your readers, and yourself. If you write for yourself, to express your own vision, you improve your craft, you challenge your readers — and you may even create a new market.

I use the word "craft" deliberately. Writers can learn craft, but not art. Only your readers can judge whether your craft has risen to the level of art. The craft of fiction is personal, idiosyncratic, finding the universal in the particular. It becomes art when it brings readers to a new state of wakefulness and sensitivity, makes readers think and feel in new ways. If you can do that, you are offering your readers a wonderful gift. Your own work may even make you think and feel differently also.

The industry of fiction, as opposed to craft, consists of interchangeable tales about all-too-familiar characters: Luke Skywalker, Mr. Spock, Conan. Like all clichés, such tales once seemed fresh and new, but their very novelty doomed them to endless repetition. Far from making readers more wakeful or sensitive, industrial-grade fiction puts them to sleep, narrows their sensitivity down to the stock response.

I know — an old joke is new if you've never heard it before, and someone's always encountering Conan or Luke for the first time. The excitement of that moment can give you a lifelong taste for SF or fantasy and for literature in general. If so, wonderful. But formula fiction is the opposite of writing that surprises, upsets, and changes its readers. Readers who never outgrow industrial fantasy and SF seem very sad to me because they miss all but the easiest pleasures of literature.

They are even sadder if they want to become writers. They may never have read anything but formula fiction, often copies of copies of copies. They may argue the merits of this formula writer over that one, but they're like kids quarreling over whether Boston Pizza is better than Domino's, while remaining utterly ignorant of Italian cuisine.

Think about J. R. R. Tolkien, whose *Lord of the Rings* has inspired so many imitators. What they don't imitate is Tolkien himself, who read widely and then wrote a story that sprang out of his well-educated imagination. When he did take ideas or images from earlier works, such as the elves and dwarves of fairy tale and folklore, he made them vividly his own.

So one of the arguments I'm going to make is that to be a really good writer of science fiction or fantasy, you should be reading as widely and deeply outside your genre as you can. You should explore 18th-century English literature, the Latin American magic realists, the legends of Polynesia, and the plays of Aeschylus. You should read the history of the Moghul emperors of India, the sagas of medieval Iceland, and the life of physicist Richard Feynman.

Writers read, and what they write is always a commentary on what they've read. What you learn from such reading will serve you well even if you're determined to build a career as a literary "sharecropper," writing formula fiction based on someone else's ideas instead of your own.

Science fiction and fantasy spring from our love of the new and strange, not from the comfort of the old and familiar. This is why I'm not fond of the clichés that now infest both genres. The only real excuse for using such clichés is to get us into a new perception of the world — including a new perception of clichés themselves! That's why I've included links to cliché lists later on in this book.

It's also why this book often uses cliché characters and situations to illustrate technical ideas about scene construction, dialogue, and outlining. Chances are you'll instantly recognize Thewbold the Barbarian and Lieutenant Chang of the Starmarines, and they won't distract you from the concept I'm trying to explain. If they seem to you to be poking fun at genres you really love, just remember that satire usually attacks what we love but what also drives us crazy. And I have to confess that some of the hokiest, corniest genres are among my guilty pleasures. When I'm laughing at Thewbold, I'm laughing at myself.

The American poet Ezra Pound once said: "Literature is news that stays news." If your story really touches on the universal — what always happens, to everyone, everywhere — it will stay news too. People will read your science fiction when your science is obsolete, and your fantasy when real dragons are hatching in high school science projects.

And some of them, when they read your work, will dream of writing too.

THE EVOLUTION OF MYTHS INTO STORIES

I assume you want to write novels, though most of my advice applies equally to short stories. In a sense, all literature is "fractal" — that is, it has the same characteristics and complexity at any level of magnitude. A novel leads us from ignorance to awareness. So does a short story. So does a paragraph. When we finish reading even a single sentence, a word, we know more than when we started reading it.

And what we want to know is that the world makes sense, that it operates on terms that humans can understand and respond to.

Our cave-dwelling ancestors saw a world full of amazing and terrifying forces: fire, flood, lightning, snow. The seasons repeated, but not always the same way. Women gave birth, but not always to live babies. Sometimes the herds of game animals disappeared, or failed to return. Whatever caused these events must be like humans, only far greater.

Explaining the forces of life, our ancestors gave them names and personalities, and tried to deal with them as children deal with parents. Sometimes, if you said the right things and behaved yourself the way the gods wished, you had a successful hunt or a healthy baby. If you misbehaved or failed to show respect, the gods would punish you.

As we slowly learned "good behavior," each generation passed its knowledge along to its children in the form of stories about the gods. Heroes were people who behaved well and enjoyed great rewards; sometimes they even became gods themselves. Stories about such people provided examples of good behavior and how it would lead to life as we all want to live it: happily, securely, with plenty of food, warmth, and love.

So one kind of ancient story reflected our wish to live in a world close to our heart's desire. Other ancient stories portrayed a hideous world in which everything goes wrong and everyone suffers because they've misbehaved. Visions of such a world would at least frighten our ancestors into behaving well even if they didn't want to.

As societies became more complex, the powers of the gods gradually shifted into the human realm. Heroes might have godlike powers, yet be as mortal as the rest of us. We had to admire them — and we also had to obey them or their descendants, which ruling classes always found convenient. If you were a Bronze Age warrior, you got less trouble and more work from the peasants if they thought you were a god's grandson.

Still more time passed, and stories now dealt with ordinary men and women. They were set in our own world, the supernatural rarely appeared in them, but the stories still followed the old mythical patterns. The universe still rewarded virtue and punished vice; the humble were exalted, and the arrogant overthrown.

In our own time, stories often deal with people who are actually less wise and free than we ourselves are. They still act out the ancient patterns, seeking love or status, but they live in a world where such yearnings are ironic and doomed. The Greeks could tell a story about an arrogant young weaver, Arachne, turned into a spider to teach her modesty. Franz Kafka told a story about Gregor Samsa, a young clerk who turns into a cockroach for no good reason at all.

If you've read Northrop Frye's *Anatomy of Criticism,* you'll recognize that I'm paraphrasing Frye's creation myth of the origins and evolution of literature. Frye also argues that literature develops in a circular fashion. It starts in myth and evolves at last into irony — literature that pokes fun at the very stories it's telling. Then it returns to myth to renew itself.

Most people, in any era, don't want to poke fun at the myths they live by. They just want a good yarn that dramatizes those myths. When ironic literature fails to do so, it ignores a powerful human yearning; so people go back to the original forms, which have persisted in "popular" literature.

When we write science fiction and fantasy, then, we are returning to our sources. We are still trying to humanize the universe we live in: even Tolkien's ancient races, the Orcs and Ents, are recognizably like us, and H. G. Wells's invading Martians can catch cold just as we do. Enormous and incomprehensible forces still rule our world, but now they're in the hands of ordinary people — the hobbit Frodo with his ring, or Lincoln Powell, the telepathic cop in Alfred Bester's *The Demolished Man.*

THE BASIC THEME OF SF AND FANTASY: POWER

Whether you're writing SF or fantasy, your basic theme is power and how to use it. Your plot is always a political one: Who should have the power, who should rule, and on what terms? Maybe your hero is an Arachne who pays a high price for her power; maybe she's like the priestess Arha in Ursula K. Le Guin's *The Tombs of Atuan* and *Tehanu,* who abandons her power for the sake of love.

If power is your basic theme, your story — whether a 500-word short story or an epic trilogy — is "anecdotal evidence" for your particular mythic vision of the world. You are telling us about how the world works in human terms, what kinds of hazards and personal flaws can subvert good behavior, and what kinds of values best inspire such behavior. Your story may take place in a gaudy world of demons and elves or on a satellite of a gas-giant planet 50,000 light-years from here — but it is still a comment about the here and now.

So let us look at the problems you as a writer must overcome.

Part 1:
Knowing Your Genre

1

Hard Facts for First-Time Novelists

You're better off understanding the challenge before you get into this business, rather than being disappointed later. So let's look at the obstacles you face as an unpublished writer trying to break into a very tough market. What follows is a chronology of an extremely lucky first novel, from inspiration to final royalty check.

October 13, 2008: You get a brilliant idea for a novel and begin writing at the rate of 1,000 finished words a day (about four double-spaced manuscript pages). You call the novel *Dragonstar.*

January 13, 2009: Now, three months later, you complete *Dragonstar.* The manuscript runs to 90,000 words (about 350 typed pages).

January 14–21, 2009: You carefully proofread before mailing the manuscript to a publisher on January 21.

January 28, 2009: *Dragonstar* arrives and happens to catch the eye of a senior editor as she passes by the slush pile, where unsolicited manuscripts usually await scanning and rejection by a junior editor. Your first page hooks her; she drops her other projects and takes your manuscript home with her.

February 1, 2009: The editor phones you, says she loves *Dragonstar,* wants to publish the book, and will send you a confirming letter.

February 15, 2009: The letter and contract arrive by courier. The letter is flattering but lists a lot of changes you should make. The offer is an advance of $5,000 against royalties based on 10 percent of the list price of a hardback edition, and a 50-50 split on the sale of paperback rights (if any). You read, sign, and return the contract by courier the same day.

February 16–March 30, 2009: You revise *Dragonstar* according to the requests in the editor's letter, and courier the revised manuscript back to her.

April 30, 2009: First installment of advance arrives: $1,666.66 (one-third of advance payable on signing contract).

July 1, 2009: Second installment of advance arrives: $1,666.66 (payable on receipt of acceptable revised manuscript).

December 31, 2009: This is the earliest possible publication date — too late for the Christmas market. Your publisher postpones *Dragonstar* to the fall of 2010 and schedules further editing and production accordingly. Meanwhile the publisher is trying to find a paperback house willing to buy the rights. So far, no takers.

April 1–4, 2010: The page proofs — the photocopies of the book's typeset pages — arrive. You proofread quickly, marveling at how much like a book your story now seems, and you return corrected pages by courier.

May 1, 2010: Your publisher holds a meeting with his sales reps to discuss the new fall catalogue, which mentions *Dragonstar.* As a first novel, your book doesn't draw much interest. But the sales reps will mention it when they talk to booksellers. At about this time you see the cover art and dust-jacket blurb, but you have no say about them; only very big-name authors can influence their books' appearance. Fortunately, you like both.

October 1, 2010: *Dragonstar*'s publication day! Books have been off the press for weeks; the "pub date" is the day by which copies should be in all the stores that have ordered it. You receive ten copies free. You can buy more at a 40 percent discount.

October 15, 2010: You receive the final third of your advance: $1,666.67 (payable on publication). By the way, your publisher has one of the fastest accounting departments in the history of Western literature.

April 1, 2011: You get your first royalty statement: between October 1 and December 31, *Dragonstar* has sold 300 copies at $30 each. Your royalty is $900, applied against your advance.

October 1, 2011: You receive your second royalty statement: between January 1 and June 30, your novel has sold another 2,200 copies. Your total royalty so far is $7,500: you receive a check for $2,500. Congratulations! You have not only "earned out" your advance, you have made additional money — a remarkable achievement for a first novelist anywhere, in any genre.

October 15, 2011: Good news! A paperback house offers $12,000 for your novel.

December 1, 2011: You and your original publisher sign the contract for the paperback. Your share is $6,000, half of it payable on signing the contract and half on publication.

February 1, 2012: You receive a check for $3,000.

April 1, 2012: The latest royalty statement on the hardback edition tells you your novel has sold 33 more copies. You receive a check for $99.

April 15, 2012: Your publisher takes the hardback edition out of print, selling the remaining copies to a jobber for $1 each; you don't receive any money from this remaindering, but you will be able to buy copies at the same price. On the remainder table, the book will sell for $4.95.

September 15, 2012: The paperback edition appears. You hate the cover.

October 13, 2012: Exactly four years after you got your inspiration and began writing, you receive a second check from the paperback house, again for $3,000. This is the last money you will see from the novel. The paperback publisher hasn't even printed enough copies to earn out your advance — she'd rather wait and see if booksellers reorder. They don't, and your novel is out of print by Christmas.

This is a very optimistic scenario for a first novel by an unknown writer. Your own experience is likely to be much tougher and more protracted.

You have this consolation: your publisher is likely to respond very quickly to your next novel, and if it's a good one, you can look forward to considerable editorial encouragement. You may even sell it on the basis of just an outline and some sample chapters. If your first two or three books sell reasonably well, advances for later ones will improve. Paperback advances may also be more generous. The publisher may even budget for serious marketing.

Nevertheless, building a career as a novelist is like building a pension fund. You are sacrificing today in hope of success several years from now. And just as you could die before you retire, you have no guarantee at all that you will succeed as a writer.

Consider some other discouraging facts: Hardback publishers throughout the English-speaking world have been losing money on "midlist" books for years. Such books used to be the bread and butter of publishing; they didn't sell in huge numbers, but they sold steadily and stayed in print for a long time. Readers got a chance to discover them years after the publication date.

But now hardback houses want blockbusters, novels that will sell scores of thousands of copies within a few weeks of publication day. Without such instant sales, booksellers will simply return the unsold copies they'd ordered — often within weeks or even days of delivery. That gives them credit toward the next batch of books they order from the same publisher, but it doesn't do the publisher any good. He or she now has to find another bookseller willing to take the copies that the first bookseller couldn't move. And returns do you, the author, even less good.

If you're working in a genre like science fiction or fantasy, you soon learn that hardback publication is largely for the big names. Readers are loyal to authors they like, and cautious about authors they don't know. If they buy a hardback SF or fantasy novel, it's going to be by an author they know and love. If they're going to gamble on an unfamiliar name like yours, they'd prefer to bet just the cost of a mass-market paperback.

 MASS MARKET? TRADE PAPERBACK?

"Mass market" means distribution through supermarkets, drugstores, and newsstands, as well as regular bookstores; "trade books" sell primarily in bookstores. A "trade paperback" is usually the size of a hardback book but with a paper cover and a price halfway between mass market and hardback.

The mass market, however, is another jungle. With hundreds of titles coming out every month, rack space is precious and every new book must earn its keep. If it doesn't, the local seller doesn't even bother to return the books — just the torn-off covers, while the books themselves go in the dumpster. (It's illegal to sell coverless books, but evidently some people do it or today's paperbacks wouldn't carry warnings about buying them.)

I once saw a drugstore clerk ripping covers off books, and as a paperback writer I took a morbid interest in what she was doing. I asked her how long she left paperback books on the racks before disposing of them. "Some of them never get out of the shipping box," she told me.

So mass-market publishers of science fiction and fantasy rarely print enough copies even to cover the cost of your advance (and they're very reluctant to tell you how many copies they've printed, because they know you can do the arithmetic). They're gambling that your *Dragonstar* will attract enough buyers to make the distributor order more copies. Reorders are essential to your book's success, and most mass-market SF and fantasy titles don't get reordered.

If this doesn't make sense, just recall that a handful of major best-selling authors are making huge profits for their publishers. The publishers invest part of those profits in buying your manuscript in the hope that you might turn out to be the next William Gibson or Robert Jordan. If you do, then some of the profits will help grubstake the next generation of writers. If you don't, you'll find it becomes harder and harder to sell later books.

In genre fiction, especially with mass-market titles, marketing is almost nonexistent. The publisher may buy a few advertisements in trade magazines such as *Locus* (which serves the SF industry — see www.locusmag.com), and may put the first chapter of your book on its website so that potential buyers can see if they like it. Reviews are few, and in any case have very little effect on mass-market sales. Your book may live or die on the strength of its cover. That's because most consumers do indeed judge a book by its cover, and they buy the cover that attracts them. The book jobbers who fill the racks do the same thing.

As the *Dragonstar* timetable above implies, actually writing the novel can be the least time-consuming part of the process. But if you take years to get your novel into publishable shape, you are only delaying the payoff even longer. As an efficient craftsperson, you should know how to complete a salable manuscript with little or no revision, and then how to get it to the right market as quickly as possible. In the next few chapters, we'll look at ways to improve your craft before turning to the issues of marketing.

2

The Past, Present, and Future of Science Fiction and Fantasy

Even if the "backstory" doesn't appear in your story, you should have a good idea of what's happened before Chapter 1 starts. For the same reason, you will write more effectively if you know something about the history of the genres of science fiction and fantasy, and if you think about how they may change in the foreseeable future. So before we get into technical details, let's survey where these genres have come from, and where they're likely to go.

Science fiction goes back a long way; the first story about a journey to the moon appeared in the 2nd century AD. Very early, one key SF element appeared; we now call this the "what if" element. What would we find if we could fly to the moon? What if sorcery worked? What if 20 billion people were living on this planet? In this kind of story, ideas are vitally important; character is less so. The stock figure is the obsessed philosopher or mad scientist who is more concerned with the ideas under discussion than with the "real" world around him. So even as SF emerged as a literature of ideas, it couldn't resist poking fun at those ideas through satire.

CONVENTIONS IN SCIENCE FICTION AND FANTASY

A genre is defined by its *conventions:* characters, settings, or events that readers expect to find in it. An attractive, difficult, unmarried man is a convention of romance. A ranch in danger is a convention of the western. An interstellar political system is a convention of SF. By the 16th or 17th century, early science fiction had developed a number of conventions, most of which are still visible in modern SF.

An Isolated Society

An isolated society could be on an island or remote mountain region that is very difficult to reach. It is often portrayed as the geographical equivalent of a womb, which may or may not be an agreeable place. Utopia, St. Thomas More tells us, resulted from the cutting of a canal across a phallic peninsula, creating a island that looks like a uterus: all the major cities are on the shores of an inland sea, which travelers enter through a narrow and dangerous strait.

Nineteenth-century novelist Samuel Butler makes entry to his Utopia, *Erewhon,* similarly difficult, as does Aldous Huxley in *Island.* In *Nineteen Eighty-Four,* George Orwell puts the secrets of Oceania in Room 101, 101 being a number that Orwell consciously intended as a female genital image.

In modern SF the isolated society may be on a colony planet, a parallel world, or a generation ship creeping between the stars. In a fantasy story the society may be isolated in time, like Middle Earth or Conan's Hyborian Age. Or it may be somehow cut off from the world around it, like Ursula K. Le Guin's Oregon town that skips around the state, thereby avoiding the blight of strip malls and fast-food joints. But in SF and fantasy we still find something uterine and comfortable about such settings. Hobbit holes are highly womblike, and Le Guin's town sounds like a great place to settle down — if that's the right term for such a highly mobile community!

In your writing, the isolated society doesn't have to be a lost colony. It could be a minority group, for example, that supports its members and defends them against outside threats. Or it could be a family — traditional or unusual — living physically or culturally apart from other people.

A Morally Significant Language

More's Utopians speak a combination of Greek and Latin, suggesting they have gone as far as non-Christian society can hope to. Orwell's Oceanians are gradually learning to speak Newspeak, designed to suppress conscious thought. In the remarkable 19th-century Canadian novel *A Strange Manuscript Found in a Copper Cylinder,* James De Mille presents an Antarctic dystopia whose inhabitants speak Hebrew. They are descendants of the Ten Lost Tribes of Israel, and their society is a grotesque perversion of Judeo-Christian values. (For a detailed discussion of this remarkable novel, see my critical essay on the CD.) And in *Cat's Cradle,* Kurt Vonnegut gives the island of San Lorenzo a degraded dialect of English.

Tolkien, of course, is the master here. His training and scholarship in languages enabled him to create languages whose moral significance lies in their esthetic qualities: Elvish Quenya, an ancient tongue of elves in *The Lord of the Rings,* is like music, while the language of the Orcs is as harsh and ugly as the Orcs themselves.

You don't have to invent your own languages, but your use of language should be very conscious. If your story portrays an oppressive bureaucracy, let us hear the bureaucrats mumbling in euphemisms and bafflegab while your hero speaks plain, blunt English.

The Importance of Documents

Science fiction writers will shut down their plots at a moment's notice if they can introduce a long extract from some important written work or other. The long epigraphs in Frank Herbert's *Dune* are an example. The Book of Bokonon, in *Cat's Cradle,* is another. In Orwell's *Nineteen Eighty-Four* Winston Smith spends considerable time reading *The Theory and Practice of Oligarchical Collectivism,* a subversive book that explains (to us more than to Winston) how Oceania has become what it is. Ursula K. Le Guin's *Always Coming Home* is an anthology of such documents, almost entirely concealing the plot.

Lacking such a document, SF characters will talk endlessly about their society and technology; sometimes the book itself, like Margaret Atwood's *The Handmaid's Tale*, is a document under discussion by academics some time in the future.

This doesn't mean you have to drag in some mythical document whether the story needs it or not. Early satirical science fiction came out of a print-based medium; its chief target is the scholar who understands (and misunderstands) the world through reading books. Your high-tech future may have abandoned print on paper altogether, and your critical document could be, for example, a new computer protocol that gives users instant access to any data bank in the world.

A Rationalist/Ideological Attitude toward Sex

Brave New World, Nineteen Eighty-Four, The Left Hand of Darkness, and many other novels express and explore a rationalist or ideological attitude toward sex. Some approve; some don't. In Yevgeny Zamyatin's novel *We*, which inspired both Huxley and Orwell, any citizen can demand sexual services from any other citizen. Huxley's young women wear their Malthusian belts, while Orwell's belong to the Anti-Sex League.

As sexual roles and expectations have changed, this aspect of SF and fantasy has changed with it. We have female soldiers in Joe Haldeman's *The Forever War* and so many female warriors in fantasy that at least one anthology parodied the practice with *Chicks in Chainmail.*

How does this affect your writing? Well, you could portray a society with what you consider ideal sexual relationships. Or you could show us relationships that are far from ideal but imposed on the characters by the kind of world you've put them in. (In Alfred

Bester's *The Stars My Destination,* many women have to be kept in labyrinths to protect them from teleporting rapists.) The distorted relationship itself becomes a criticism of your world's social order. Changing that social order will mean not only justice and freedom but also improved relations between men and women.

An Inquisitive Outsider

Genly Ai in *The Left Hand of Darkness,* Gulliver in his *Travels,* and countless others serve as lenses through which we observe "what if" societies. Their own cultural biases may influence their perceptions, but they often see that the culture they are studying is in some way only their own with some aspect exaggerated or diminished. (In some cases, as with Gulliver or Winston Smith, we may understand this better than the narrator. When that happens, we are dealing with irony.)

In your writing, the inquisitive outsider may be your central character, but he or she doesn't have to come from somewhere else. Your hero may be a teenage girl who's trying to understand why her lunar-colony society has a taboo against going out on the surface, or a young soldier trying to pull back from the gritty details of combat training to learn the real causes of the war he's supposed to fight.

The Fusion of Satire and Romance

Renaissance science fiction, as a literature of ideas, was never a "popular" genre. More's *Utopia* circulated among a small circle of intellectuals. But other writers soon found they could use elements from science fiction in popular fiction — which had always been fond of monsters, strange kingdoms, and exotic locales. This kind of "romance" gave us a brave hero (often aristocratic but reared in obscurity), wise old men, evil usurpers, perilous quests, and an essentially conservative political agenda: the hero's job is usually to preserve or restore an idealized feudal society.

Interest in romance grew throughout the great age of European exploration, discovery, and conquest. Adventurers encountered lands and societies that seemed like something out of popular fiction; when the conquistadors first saw Tenochtitlán, the Aztecs' imperial capital, one of them said that it was like something out of *Amadis of Gaul* — a medieval thriller.

While the typical European response to these new societies was to try to destroy them, they nevertheless posed a challenge that many thinkers and writers were glad to meet. Europeans saw that different peoples had found different solutions to the problems of organizing themselves; society was therefore not so much God-ordained as humanly designed. The dangerous implication here was that we might actually implement ideas to change our own society, rather than imposing change only by force of arms.

The debate raged on for centuries: What is the real nature of man — fallen angel, noble savage, decayed child of great ancestors, or ancestor of wiser, greater descendants? In the light of foreign societies, Europeans criticized their own, and some critics paid a high price. So it became safer to write satire, poking fun at the follies of mythical societies, than to poke fun at the follies of one's own society.

In hindsight, the European encounter with the rest of the world was enormously stimulating to the Europeans — though often fatal to everyone else. As the age of exploration and conquest ended, literature kept on offering fictional versions of what had been factual accounts. Ever since Columbus, Cortés, and Pizarro, Europeans had been discovering new worlds and lost civilizations; by the mid-19th century, however, authors had few blank spots left on the map, while readers continued to demand at least fictional discoveries.

It's not surprising, then, that authors took readers deep into the jungles of Africa and South America, or into the mountain valleys of Tibet, to find new societies, strange creatures, and magical lore. Others began to look to other worlds, or to the future, simply because the 19th century had run out of the right kind of real estate.

So what we often consider the dawn of science fiction — the age of Jules Verne and H. G. Wells — was really the high noon of a long-established genre. The contribution of Verne and Wells was to define the major subgenres; I'm not sure if anyone since has actually created a new kind of SF story that owes nothing to them.

The Evolution of Fantasy

Meanwhile, fantasy was beginning to evolve into a genre of its own, after centuries of being just another kind of story about remote and wonderful places. In many ways it was an understandable reaction against the changes that science in the service of industrialism was making to traditional society. William Blake's "dark Satanic mills" had cut people off from their roots; the old stories let them tap into a lost past.

Folktales and fairy tales blithely portrayed a world of witches and spells even while it was thought that science was driving superstition from the public mind; by the 19th century these tales had become common childhood reading thanks to Hans Christian Andersen and the Grimm brothers. Authors brought up on such stories began to experiment with them, creating genuine literary works out of the imagery and motifs of fairy tale. Writers such as William Morris, consciously rejecting industrial society, created quasi-medieval worlds in which magic worked, and readers responded very happily to these worlds.

In the early 20th century, a number of writers like Lord Dunsany, "Saki" (the pen name of H. H. Munro), and E. R. Eddison enriched the genre. Sometimes, like Eddison, they set their fantasy worlds in "real" places, like the planet Mercury, but with no effort to make these settings resemble those worlds as astronomers knew them.

So when J. R. R. Tolkien published *The Lord of the Rings* in the 1950s, he was working in a familiar genre — but on a scale never before seen. Readers came to him after reading H. P. Lovecraft, Saki, C. S. Lewis, and other fantasy writers, but Tolkien's scope and vision changed the genre forever — not always for the better.

Those of us writing SF and fantasy now face a serious problem:

we find it hard to say anything new in genres that rely for their impact on the novelty of their ideas. Moreover, SF and fantasy are so market-driven that genuine originality is likely to languish in the slush pile.

At the same time we realize that both genres are really about the here and now, not some magical realm or the far future: Isaac Asimov's *Foundation* series, for example, is really about the uncertainties of the post-World War II international order. *The Left Hand of Darkness* is largely about the changing sexual mores of the 1960s. Tolkien was attacking totalitarianism and the more brutal aspects of the industrial era.

Given the current pace of events, however, it's hard to find a "present" that isn't ancient history by the time we've dealt with it in print. (Think of all those versions of World War III fought against the Soviet Union.)

We writers therefore face an awkward choice: Accept the conventions of this or that subgenre (military SF, time-traveling police, space opera, cyberpunk, sword and sorcery) and write more or less academic exercises on their themes. Or we can try to turn our chosen genres on their heads.

Satirizing SF and fantasy can work up to a point (after all, they themselves are forms of satire), but it's also a sign that the original genre has run out of energy. Terry Pratchett's Discworld tales are a hoot at first, but after a dozen titles even loyal readers may find the gags a bit stale. And part of the appeal of both genres is that old reliable — the sense of wonder. We want the elation and excitement of romance, the sense of awe in encountering the mysterious, as well as the intellectual amusement of satire.

WHERE DO WE GO FROM HERE?

I suspect that future SF and fantasy will find most scope in two divergent directions.

The first of these will be *superrealism,* or "bottom line" stories. In science fiction, bottom-line writers will explore economically viable societies and the uses they make of science and technology. So no more *Star Wars* stories unless the authors show how you can pay for interstellar warfare — and what its benefits are. No more societies ruled by megacorporations unless you can show how such groups develop a genuine advantage over public institutions. By showing how economic or political principles rule future societies, we can examine how those principles rule our own.

In fantasy, the bottom-line approach will encourage writers who want to drag the genre out of the Middle Ages. Walter Jon Williams's *Metropolitan* novels, set in an urban world running on "plasm," are a welcome step in this direction.

The second direction might be called *antirealism* or (to coin a pompous literary criticism term) "mythotropic" literature — stories that move toward myth. Sir Arthur C. Clarke has argued that technology, if advanced enough, is indistinguishable from magic. So in mythotropic SF we assume a Clarkean level of technology that, by becoming magic, enables its users to act out whatever their inmost desires might be — to behave, in effect, like gods or demons. Just as myth enables us to humanize the world we encounter, mythotropic SF would enable us to explore our own psyches on a grand scale.

Mythotropic fantasy, by contrast, would use the common images (dragons, swords, caves, forests) as conscious metaphors for aspects of the human mind and experience; it would also explore other cultural traditions with unfamiliar myths and images, seeking both exotic novelty and whatever is common to all cultures in their response to the human condition.

Both kinds of literature would still, of course, be about ourselves at the turn of the millennium.

But if we can see the essential pattern in technological change, and the psychological constants in our images of fantasy, our fiction will have a better chance of lasting, of appealing to readers growing up in a very real 21st century.

RELATED READING

In addition to the novels and authors mentioned in this chapter, I strongly recommend that you explore the origins of all Western literature: the Bible, Homer's *Iliad* and *Odyssey*, Greek drama, Roman verse, and nonfiction. A taste of Asian literatures could also inspire some useful ideas: the *Ramayana* of India, Chinese novels like *The Journey to the West*, or medieval Japanese classics like *The Tale of Genji*. You will be pleasantly surprised at how much like SF and fantasy they are.

The literary studies of the late Canadian scholar Northrop Frye, especially his *Anatomy of Criticism* and *The Secular Scripture*, provide a very useful context for science fiction and fantasy; our genres deal in myth and archetype, and no one understands them better than Frye. Studies in comparative mythology, like Joseph Campbell's *Hero with a Thousand Faces*, can also offer guidance.

3

Understanding Genre

"Genre" simply means a kind of literature (usually fiction) dealing with a particular topic, setting, or issue. Even so-called mainstream fiction has its subgenres: the coming-of-age story, for example, and the *bildungsroman* — about the education, formal and otherwise, of the main character.

In the last few decades, genre in North America has become synonymous with "category" — types of fiction that are commercially successful because they are predictable treatments of familiar material: the Regency romance, the hard-boiled detective novel, the space opera.

This has made "genre" something of a dirty word. Some readers, writers, and critics dismiss genre or category fiction precisely because of its predictability, and they're often right to do so.

But even the humblest hackwork requires a certain level of craft, and that means you must understand your genre's conventions if you are going to succeed — and especially if you are going to convey your message by tinkering with those conventions.

DEFINING OUR TERMS

First, a couple of quick definitions. A science fiction story is one in which the story couldn't happen without its scientific content. The story can't contradict what we currently accept as scientific fact, such as the impossibility of going faster than light, but it can speculate on what may turn out to be fact — such as a way to travel through some other kind of space where the speed of light is not a factor.

A fantasy story is one in which the conditions are flatly contrary to scientific fact. Magic works. Supernatural beings intervene in human affairs. People have destinies, often foretold long before their birth.

In either genre, the basics of storytelling still apply. The characters are moving from a state of ignorance to a state of knowledge, and defining their identities by their actions.

A mainstream story is anecdotal evidence for a belief about the way the real world operates — what critics would call a "mythic vision." It's a way of saying, "See what happens when people fall in love in Iowa in the 1990s?" "See what happens when a hard-working immigrant tries to adjust to life in 21st-century Canada?"

A science fiction or fantasy story provides similar evidence for a mythic vision of a world we imagine living in. If people fall in love on Mars, or in Middle Earth, does the relationship work in some different way from our own world? If a society is in danger on Capella IV or in Lyonesse, can a hero rescue it?

The usual answer seems to be that life on Mars or Middle Earth will be comfortingly similar but entertainingly different. People will drink beer while admiring double-star sunsets. They will battle for personal freedom against alien or demonic oppressors. They will teleport to Andromeda, enjoying the wonder of it as we do not when we board the red-eye flight from Los Angeles to New York.

This is both an advantage and a pitfall for you as a writer of SF or fantasy. You can enjoy writing about a flirtation aboard an interstellar ship as much as earlier writers did about romances on Atlantic liners. But you may also make your fantasy or future worlds just a little too cozy and similar to our own — when the whole purpose of the genres is to show us the familiar in a context of the new, the strange, and the wonderful.

You may love science fiction or fantasy, but no one declares a passion for "mainstream" fiction. Mainstream is the term used by writers and readers of category fiction to describe whatever doesn't fit in a category — especially realistic fiction set in the present or recent past. A story about a young woman becoming a sorcerer is fantasy. A young woman becoming a warp-drive engineer is science fiction. A young woman becoming a teacher in 1950's Iowa is mainstream.

UNDERSTANDING THE CONVENTIONS OF YOUR GENRE

For our purposes, a *convention* is an understanding between writer and reader about certain details of the story. For example, we don't need to know the detailed history of 21st-century space exploration to understand why your hero is prospecting in the Asteroid Belt in 2089. We don't need to understand the post-Einstein physics that permits faster-than-light travel and the establishment of interstellar empires. And we usually agree that the hero of a sword and sorcery novel should be heterosexual, unmarried, and pretty good at hand-to-hand combat. (Although gay and lesbian heroes are challenging this convention.)

As a novice writer, you should understand your genre's conventions consciously, not just as things you take for granted that help make a good yarn. In this, you're like an apprentice cook. You can't just uncritically love the taste of tomato soup; you have to know what ingredients and treatment make it taste that way, and use them with some calculation.

It might be useful for you to write out your own understanding and appreciation of the form you're working in. I found this was especially helpful with a couple of my early books, *Icequake* and *Tsunami,* which fell into the subgenre of the world-disaster thriller. Because I didn't fully understand the conventions of the genre, in an early draft of *Icequake* I wasted too much time introducing the characters and watching them interact.

My editor and I agreed the novel was far too slow at the start, so I chopped the first 60 pages and replaced them with just 25, bringing the disaster as close to the start of the story as I could. Then, to clarify what I'd learned, I wrote a brief description of thriller conventions. I wish I'd done that first!

Your genre analysis doesn't have to be in essay form; it just has to identify the key elements of the genre as you understand them, and that in turn should lead to ideas about how to tinker with the genre's conventions. And *that,* in turn, should make your story more interesting than a slavish imitation of your favorite author.

As an example, here are my own views about the thriller in general and the disaster thriller in particular:

(a) The thriller portrays persons confronting problems they can't solve by recourse to established institutions and agencies; calling the local emergency telephone number or a psychiatrist won't help matters in the slightest.

(b) The problems not only threaten the characters' physical and mental safety, they threaten to bring down the society they live in: their families, their communities, their nations. This is what is at stake in the story, and should appear as soon as possible.

(c) The solution to the characters' problems usually involves some degree of violence, illegality, technical expertise, and dramatic action, but not more than we can plausibly expect from people of the kind we have chosen to portray.

(d) The political thriller portrays characters who must go outside their society if they are to save it, and the characters therefore acquire a certain ironic quality. They must be at least as skilled and ruthless as their adversaries, yet motivated by values we can understand and admire even if we don't share them.

(e) The disaster thriller portrays characters who are either isolated from their society or who risk such isolation if they fail. That is, either they will die or their society will fall (or both) if they do not accomplish their goals.

In the novel of natural disaster, the disaster comes early and the issue is who will survive and how. In the novel of human-caused disaster, the issue is how (or whether) the characters will prevent the disaster — which, if it happens, must happen very late in the story. (However, the novel *Icefire,* by Judith and Garfield Reeves-Stevens, twists this convention: the disaster happens relatively early in the story, and causes death and destruction for several hundred pages, and the story then hinges on whether the disaster can be halted before it affects North America.)

(f) The characters must be highly plausible and complex; where they seem grotesque or two-dimensional, we must give some valid reason for these qualities. They must have adequate motives for the extreme and risky actions they take, and they must respond to events with plausible human reactions. Those reactions should spring from what we know of the characters' personalities, and should throw new light on those personalities.

(g) The protagonist's goal is to save a threatened society (Walter Tevis's *The Man Who Fell to Earth*) or to restore a vanquished one (Robert Heinlein's *Sixth Column*); it is rarely to create a whole new society. (But see Heinlein's *The Moon Is a Harsh Mistress* as a notable exception.)

(h) At the outset the protagonist only reacts to events; at some point, however, he or she embarks on the "counterthrust," an attempt to take charge and overcome circumstances.

(i) The progress of the protagonist is from ignorance to knowledge, accomplished through a series of increasingly intense and important conflicts. In the human-caused disaster, the conflicts are likely to be with other people. In the natural disaster, the conflicts are with the environment itself, and only marginally with other people. These struggles lead to a climactic conflict and the resolution of the story.

(j) With the climax, the protagonist attains self-knowledge as well as understanding of his or her circumstances (or at least the readers attain such knowledge). This knowledge may well create a whole new perspective on the story's events and the characters' values: a murder may turn out to have been futile, or loyalty may have been betrayed. We should prepare for these insights early in the novel, so that the protagonist's change and development are logical and believable.

THE SUBGENRES OF SCIENCE FICTION

To a striking degree, the common science fiction subgenres repeat the history of only the past thousand years or so: the rise and fall of empires, the discovery of new lands and peoples, the founding of new nations, the invention of new technologies. (I think it was Frank Herbert, long ago, who retold the Spanish conquest of Peru as a straight SF story.)

Clearly these subgenres remain popular precisely because we have something in history to compare them with. But I suggest that if you choose one or more of them as the basis of your story, you should deliberately try to push the limits in some way. Otherwise you risk lapsing into cliché and stereotype, and you invite harsh comparison with the earlier writers who did it before and did it

better. Here are my own admittedly crabby opinions on some standard kinds of SF tales and the cliché hazards they pose.

Hard Science Fiction

Hard science fiction is the domain of the physicist and engineer; the story depends for its success on a clear, thorough understanding of present-day science as well as its implications. If you want to set your story on a comet in the Oort Cloud, or in the core of a star about to go supernova, you'd better know your stuff; your readers certainly will.

You'd also better know how to camouflage your stuff; a hard-SF story is still a story, and long expository passages can kill reader interest in seconds. While dialogue is often a useful way to convey some exposition, in hard science fiction the results range from stupefying to unintentionally funny: "Well, Fred, as we all learned in grad school back on Vega II, extreme plasma density in a pre-supernova stellar core creates semitensility within 1,000 miles of the chromosphere, which means that from now on we'll have to use a lead-based sunblock."

If you're not well trained in current science, this is not a sub-genre to pursue. You're likely to make too many mistakes in basic science, never mind the rarefied physics of a triple-star solar system or the metabolism of a being with quadruple-strand DNA. And if you are scientifically well trained, give a bottom-line thought to the society that funds all those expeditions to neutron stars and black holes. What are the taxpayers getting out of it? Even a hard-science story has a political aspect.

Alien Invasion

The science fiction subgenre of alien invasion requires too many coincidences: to be of any use as enemies, the aliens have to be able to live on a planet like ours, have to be about our size, have to travel in spacecraft, have to be technologically advanced but not impossibly so, have to be able to communicate in ways we can at least guess at, and have to act on intelligible motivation.

What's more, they have to be willing to schlep across interstellar space and lower themselves into our gravity well just so they can beat us up and take over an ecosystem they probably know almost nothing about.

In other words, we're just looking at the European conquest of the Americas all over again, only from the Indians' point of view. Such tales are usually pretty boring, because the authors of such tales haven't extended their imaginations enough. Suppose the aliens have invaded repeatedly, and were superior to us as we are to ants. Would we even know they were here? Would Peruvian ants know, or care, that the Spanish had arrived? And did the Spanish try to conquer the ants?

The worst cliché in this outworn category is the story about the collectivist, "hive-mind" species that wants to take us over. Rugged, individualist humans somehow always outsmart the technologically advanced hive-mind, with the noise of grinding axes in the background. These stories were common during the Cold War, when the hive-mind was an obvious metaphor for communism. When they turn up now, they're about as interesting as a stale bagel.

So if you must do an alien-invasion story, make the aliens as strange as possible.

Alien Contact

If the aliens aren't aggressive, they're still out there somewhere; maybe they land in an Iowa cornfield, or we meet them orbiting Sirius XI. The story then revolves around efforts to communicate, to empathize with nonhuman ways of thinking, and to avoid a disastrous misunderstanding.

This has been done to death, but its appeal persists. Perhaps that's why "factual" books about alien abductions and crashed flying saucers are so popular.

Again I suggest making your aliens as alien as possible. Stanislaw Lem pointed the way in his novel *Solaris,* where the alien "ocean" has nothing in common with us but a desire to understand and communicate. If you bring in spindly, lovable little aliens with big eyes, you'd better do so with ironic intent.

This is not to demand weirdness for its own sake, but to stretch the definition of human well beyond dear old E.T. If an alien ocean wants to communicate with us, and we can understand its intent, then the alien is another aspect of humanity and the universe is a more understandable place.

Interstellar Empire

Hundreds of science fiction writers (of European descent) have imagined that the social institutions of medieval Europe would be beautifully adaptable to running interstellar empires. All those dukes and counts and imperial highnesses look romantic to us North Americans — many of us descended, of course, from peasants eager to escape their aristocratic masters.

So this subgenre can easily be mere romanticism — a weak basis for a solid story. More to the point, few interstellar empires ever have much economic or social reason for existence. If bottom-line SF, or superrealism, does emerge as I hope it will, all those empires and foundations will go the way of Troy and Babylon, and not a minute too soon.

Interstellar War

A generation of science fiction writers grew up in the 1950s watching *Victory at Sea,* a documentary series about the U.S. Navy in World War II, on their old black-and-white television sets. Now we get endless dreary interstellar wars waged for no reason, and fought by "fleets" commanded by "admirals" who maneuver in three-dimensional space as if they were cruising the South Pacific.

Star Trek is the most influential of these tales, because it has sunk its roots deepest in readers' and viewers' imaginations. Supposedly the civilization that supports Captains Kirk, Picard, et al. has solved problems of human conflict. In that case, why has it retained the military-bureaucratic structure of the 20th century? Why doesn't Kirk show up on the bridge in jeans and a T-shirt? For that matter, why not run the ship from his cabin? He doesn't really need to speak face to face with Mr. Spock; the intercom system works well enough between the bridge and the engine room, after all.

Trekkies may argue that humanity still has to battle some alien species, but it seems daft to do so with a military system of the distant past — as if Admiral Nimitz could have beaten the Japanese by behaving like Captain Bligh, shanghaiing his sailors and then flogging them for breaking regulations.

If you must write about interstellar war, give us plausible reasons for fighting across such distances. The best I could manage in my novel *Gryphon* was a species locked in a kind of mass religious psychosis; they believed they had to go forth and convert the heathen in person, not just by interstellar signals. I hope your novel offers something better.

Your warfare, by the way, ought to be highly catastrophic. Anyone controlling enough energy to cross several light-years should be able to turn any planet into talcum powder. But even Robert Heinlein's evil Bugs, in *Starship Troopers,* could only knock out Buenos Aires. At interstellar distances that's like launching an intercontinental missile with a firecracker for a warhead.

Space Opera

Whether interplanetary or interstellar, the space opera subgenre is simply interested in living — and making a living — in space. War or aliens are often involved, but needn't be. Often the space opera deals with small traders trying to keep up the mortgage on their battered old freighter while the big companies (or interstellar empires) threaten to drive them out of business. While planets may be ports of call, space opera's main settings are artificial: spacefaring freighters, warships, scout vessels, orbiting docks.

Related subgenres include the space habitat (thousands or millions of people living in a single gigantic orbiting craft, sometimes a hollow planetoid, more often an artificial cylinder) and the generation ship (a self-sustaining interstellar craft taking hundreds of years to travel between stars).

Personally, I'd be a lot more interested in the economies of planets that could afford to pay the freight charges on cargoes transported over several light-years. What are those folks on the surface doing that's so profitable? If as a reader I'm interested in such questions, then I hope you, as a writer, are ready to answer them.

The Colony

Countless science fiction writers have cheerfully plagiarized the settlement of America by putting humans on Mars, Venus, or some imaginary world. Popular examples include Kim Stanley Robinson's *Red Mars, Green Mars, Blue Mars* trilogy. The appeal of the pioneer colony story is in seeing how the combination of brains, grit, and high-tech can make a hostile planet livable — while evolving appropriate new societies.

Such societies generally break away from the mother planet, sometimes violently. That's because the pioneers are cranky, individualistic misfits who don't get along with the pompous bureaucrats back home on Earth. How did these misfits pass the psychological screening?

Heinlein's *The Moon Is a Harsh Mistress* gives us such a conflict; so does Robinson. But if they can't win against the home world, the pioneers just head farther out, like Huck Finn fleeing "sivilization." Greg Bear's *Moving Mars* pushes this escapism to a new limit: his rebel colonists move the whole planet to another solar system.

Some bold innovator in this subgenre is going to reverse the trend: Interstellar colonists will bring their planets back to the solar system, so it's less trouble for family reunions and imports will be cheaper. And imagine what the night sky will look like, with a dozen Earth-sized planets in it!

An even bolder innovator will show his or her colonists (or colonizers) developing advanced psychological techniques for conflict resolution, instead of simply finding a techno-fix permitting the oppressed colonists to run away.

The lost colony is another overdone subject, attractive because it allows some "cultural drift" to create a very different society that's still human. Conveniently, lost colonies often lose their advanced technology and people must resort to clanking around in armor with broadswords. Not all such stories are hopeless. In Ursula K. Le Guin's Hainish tales such as *The Left Hand of Darkness* and *Four Ways to Forgiveness,* Earth itself is a lost colony, newly returned to the "Ekumen," an interstellar federation of human worlds. Le Guin succeeds brilliantly at showing us a rich variety of human cultures interacting with one another in ways both familiar and strange.

Military Science Fiction

If all American literature springs from Mark Twain's *The Adventures of Huckleberry Finn,* then all military science fiction springs from Robert Heinlein's *Starship Troopers,* first published in 1959. I doubt that any of the mainstream bestsellers of that year still inspire a fraction of the debate and imitation that this novel has.

The focus in military science fiction is on the life and death of soldiers in future wars, especially in space. The mood may be pro-war (as most readers take Heinlein to be) or antiwar (as in Joe Haldeman's *The Forever War,* where an interstellar conflict is sustained for centuries by a human military establishment). But military SF concentrates on technology, training, and the kind of culture that supports (and betrays) such soldiers.

Near-Future Politics

The science fiction subgenre of near-future politics has only a hazy boundary with some kinds of mainstream fiction. A common example is the political soap opera set in the near future only for convenience, like the Allen Drury *Advise and Consent* novels of the 1950s and '60s. The hazard of this field is that your novel, like Drury's, may well be out of date before it's even published. Assuming a minimum three-year gap between starting your novel and seeing it in print, you should focus on politics at least a decade from the present.

I admit to being very cautious because of my own experience: In 1984, I started a novel about what would happen in China after the death of its leader, Deng Xiaoping. When I decided the old guy couldn't last much longer, and events would overtake my story, I junked the project. Who would have expected Deng to go on living as long as he did?

Near-Future Wars

The science fiction subgenre of near-future wars has been around for over a century. Novels like Raymond LeQueuex's *The Invasion of 1910* (published in 1906) helped create the anti-German, pro-war attitudes that sustained World War I. H. G. Wells was a master of the form, with *The War in the Air* foretelling Zeppelin raids and dogfights, while *The World Set Free* predicted atomic bombs dropped (by hand) from aircraft.

After Hiroshima, this subgenre flourished, reflecting the anxieties of a generation that had been born in one great war, fought in a second, and expected to die in a third. *On the Beach, Dark December, Farnham's Freehold,* and scores of other titles helped us think about the unthinkable. The end of the Cold War left this subgenre with no plausible enemies, but we see Islamic terrorists trying their hand at biological warfare in Daniel Kalla's *Pandemic:* having deliberately infected themselves with a nasty new virus, they then spread the disease in western airports and hotels.

Far-Future Societies

Olaf Stapledon, a British writer, pioneered the subgenre of far-future societies in *Last and First Men* and *Star Maker.* While his cosmology is out of date, his vision is still grand. Here we look at societies grown old and interestingly decayed, or perhaps new societies arising from their ashes.

As with lost colony stories, this subgenre often gives us technologically backward societies; I did so in *Eyas,* which is set in British Columbia ten million years from now, and so did Brian Aldiss in his novel *Hothouse.* The premise is that civilizations are cyclical, so if we start with a primitive society we can trace its technological progress — and, we hope, its spiritual progress as well.

The far-future story often tends to the mythotropic (see Chapter 2), portraying persons and societies acting out their deepest urges, with the scientific resources to do so. The fun arises in seeing how holding enormous power makes little difference to people who are still enslaved by the same drives that we are.

For ideas about *really* far-future stories, see the remarkable book by astrophysicists Fred Adams and Greg Laughlin, *The Five Ages of the Universe: Inside the Physics of Eternity.*

Mutants

The belief in progress led some early evolutionists to imagine that humanity was becoming better all the time and might eventually give rise to a new species far superior to our own. Olaf Stapledon's *Odd John* is a fine story reflecting this view. Nuclear weapons —

especially their radiation — inspired an endless series of mutant stories. Usually the mutation gives remarkable powers: telepathy, extrasensory perception, precognition. The mutant may pay a price, usually a social one: everyone else is scared of mutants and wants to kill them. Wilmar Shiras's novel *Children of the Atom* is a good example, showing kids with enormously high IQs who are smart enough to play dumb around ordinary people.

More recently, we've seen a new subgenre, genetic engineering, emerge. Sometimes it leads to lethal new viruses cooked up in labs; sometimes it produces superbabies who create brilliant inventions or go insane, or both. In either subgenre, the definition of "human" is a critical theme … or, in the case of Michael Crichton's *Jurassic Park,* the definition of "dinosaur."

Nanotechnology

Inspired by the thoughts of physicist K. Eric Drexler, nanotechnology foresees molecule-sized, intelligent computers that can do anything from grow house-sized diamonds to sucking the cholesterol out of your bloodstream. Science fiction authors seized on the idea. In *Gryphon,* I assumed nanotech would lead to universal wealth on a vast scale, with each individual relying on nanotech for health, transportation, and protection from other people.

The trouble with such a scenario is that the usual motivations for dramatic behavior — fear of poverty, the desire for security — become obsolete. My nanotech users had no need for society, never mind government, and would meet physically only for sex or violence. But here again we have mythotropic literature: a technology resembling magic, with its possessors behaving like immature gods.

At the time of this writing, I'm wrestling again with this problem in a novel about a nanotechnologist who finds he's not sure how or why he is being transformed into a superhuman. (See the appendix for an annotated chapter from my work in progress.)

Post-Holocaust Barbarism

Jack London and H. G. Wells long ago envisioned a world flung into backwardness — in London's case by plague, in Wells's by unrestricted air war. The nuclear weapon lent credibility to the idea of regression to barbarism, and no one knows how many such novels have explored the idea. Walter M. Miller's *A Canticle for Leibowitz* and John Wyndham's *The Chrysalids* (also published as *Re-Birth*) are literate, thoughtful explorations of the subgenre.

But when it keeps turning up in movies such as *The Road Warrior* and *The Postman,* you know it's as dead as a Norwegian Blue Parrot. If this is the kind of story you want to tell, you'll need some really original twist. Otherwise, everyone's going to consider your story as just another rehash of pretty stale material.

Does every story need a totally new idea? No. Every basic SF and fantasy idea has been done many times, and your readers are familiar with countless variations on those ideas. So the variation you come up with should be distinctly different. When Russell Hoban wrote *Riddley Walker,* yet another post-Holocaust tale, he told the whole story in the weirdly degenerate English of his future society. It was a brilliant evocation of a barbarous world.

World Disasters

John Barnes's *Mother of Storms* is an example of this subgenre, where the real hero is the disaster itself; the human characters are just there to give us a viewpoint. Others, of varying quality, include John Christopher's *The Death of Grass,* Kurt Vonnegut's *Cat's Cradle,* and Larry Niven and Jerry Pournelle's *Lucifer's Hammer.* George R. Stewart's *Earth Abides* and Jack London's *The Scarlet Plague* show us the barbaric aftermaths of horrendous pandemics.

I took two tries at this form, *Icequake* and *Tsunami;* both deal with the same event, but in different locales. It's harder than it looks.

The world disaster story gives you a chance to trash institutions and countries you don't approve of, but it may also reveal more about your social anxieties than you intend. *Lucifer's Hammer,* for example, expresses a white-suburban dread of the black ghetto that I found profoundly embarrassing: the worst aspect of being hit by a celestial object, in this novel, is that black people are going to try to survive at white suburbanites' expense.

The same was true of one of the original novels in this genre, *When Worlds Collide,* by Philip Wylie and Edwin Balmer. Published in 1932, it portrayed brilliant scientists building a nuclear rocket to carry a few survivors to a new home. But before they can escape, the scientists' base is attacked by starving, desperate people led (literally) by a charismatic man on horseback. The scientists use their rocket's exhaust to incinerate the invaders. In a novel about the colliding worlds of fascism, communism, and depression-crippled capitalism, the authors' dread of working-class people is obvious.

Utopias and Dystopias

We usually take utopia to mean an ideal society, but the last century has shown us that creating an ideal society somehow always involves shooting people who don't measure up to the ideal.

As a result, serious writing about a utopia — portraying a society the author honestly believes to be good — is relatively rare these days. When Edward Bellamy published *Looking Backward* in 1888, he described a utopian socialist America in the year 2000, complete with credit cards and music piped into people's homes by the phone company. His book started a whole political movement. But it's hard to imagine any utopian vision inspiring something similar today. (For more on this novel, see my critical essay on the CD.)

By contrast, dystopian works are flourishing. Publishers aren't usually keen to publish them — novels in which the society is inventively and ruthlessly repressive, and the hero's task is to escape it or overthrow it. Nevertheless, thousands of writers have broken into print with one warning or another — trying, in Ray Bradbury's phrase, to prevent the future.

Probably the earliest work about a modern dystopia is Jack London's 1911 novel *The Iron Heel*. London gives us a totalitarian America fought by a socialist resistance movement led by "Ernest Everhard," who to modern readers seems more like a foreshadowing of Nazism. As touched on in the previous chapter, later dystopians include Yevgeni Zamyatin (*We*), Aldous Huxley (*Brave New World*), and of course George Orwell (*Nineteen Eighty-Four* and *Animal Farm*).

These authors were seen in their time as literary satirists, not as science fiction writers. But the professional SF authors they inspired have also been brilliantly satirical. In *The Space Merchants,* by Frederik Pohl and C. M. Kornbluth, the hero escapes to Venus from an over-populated world ruled by advertising agencies. In *The Dispossessed,* Ursula K. Le Guin gives us two dystopias: an anarchist utopia gone bad and a capitalist dystopia that never even wanted to be good.

Such books are often fun, but beware of incorporating a liberation movement that wants to solve its dystopian problems by going back to the U.S. Constitution (Isaac Asimov's *The Stars, Like Dust*) or some other current document. We would not think much of a current rebel movement that wanted to rescue us by restoring the Code of Hammurabi, adopting the social structure of the Incas, or imposing the Wiccan religion on everyone. So why should we sup-pose that our political institutions and values will be suitable to the societies of the far future?

As a reader, I'd love to find a story about a 27th-century utopian movement with values very different from our own — a story that makes me root for those values.

Wild Talents: Telepathy, Teleportation, and More

Straight power-tripping: read girls' minds and find out which ones are interested (but suppose they *all* think you're a jerk?); jump instantly from home to work, or better yet to a beach in Costa Rica (but since the earth is moving faster in the latitude of Costa Rica than in the lat-itude of Chicago, the ground will instantly fly out from under your feet and you'll be pulped the next time you hit ground); or fly through the air like Superman, overcoming gravity by sheer mental power.

We've all had these fantasies, and they can be fun. I confess I've used telepathy in at least one novel, and devoted another (*Lifter*) to the problems of a levitating teenager. Again, the fun lies in exploring the unexpected aspect of our wishes. Rick Stevenson, my flying teenager, finds that when he takes his hands out of his pockets to wipe his nose, his pants slip down to his ankles. And when he tries for an altitude record, he passes out from lack of oxygen and revives barely in time to save himself.

He also worries about what will happen when gun nuts and rapists learn how to fly — and they certainly will.

When you're tempted to write about a dream come true, be sure that the dream turns into a nightmare as quickly as possible. A wild-talent story, then, should entice readers into rethinking their fantasies, and making them thank heaven that their talents are more tame.

Time Travel

Time-travel stories have explored so many logical paradoxes that they offer very few new twists. This is too bad, since physicists now seem more disposed to accept the basic idea as long as it includes a couple of black holes rotating around one another, and a solution to the awkward problem of tidal forces ripping time travelers apart.

Connecticut Yankee

One popular subgenre, the Connecticut Yankee, gives us a modern protagonist who goes back in time to start a new industrial revolution. The term comes from a Mark Twain story in which his hero, an engineer, mechanizes the court of King Arthur but his innovations lead only to a bloodbath by knights on bicycles. L. Sprague de Camp, in *Lest Darkness Fall,* sends his archaeologist hero back to 6th-century Rome, where he introduces brandy, newspapers, and stock markets.

I couldn't resist playing with this idea in *Rogue Emperor,* in which some aggressively fundamentalist Christians take over Rome in AD 100. They find the Romans impressed with firearms but not with holographic images in the Colosseum — they prefer old-fashioned gladiatorial blood and guts.

Most Connecticut Yankee stories spring from a sweet-natured but misplaced faith in technology as the solution to all problems — especially if the technology is machine guns against iron swords or AK-47s against single-shot black-powder rifles (see Harry Turtledove's *The Guns of the South*).

Yet when isolated members of technologically advanced societies have actually settled in more backward societies, they have rarely made a dent. As a real-life example, John Jewitt, a British sailor and blacksmith, was enslaved by the Nootka Indians on Vancouver Island late in the 18th century. His impact on the Nootka was limited to the iron tools he made for them, which they used to pursue their own cultural interests like war and wood carving; he certainly didn't turn them into an industrial civilization!

The moral for authors of time-travel stories: Cultures are tough organisms that recognize only the technology that suits their own values and needs.

Parallel Worlds and Alternate Histories

Parallel worlds and alternate histories are great fun too. The parallel world gives us the present (or future) resulting from some changed event in the past. The alternate history gives us an era in the past that's different because of such an event. If Napoleon had won at Waterloo, a novel about his death in Paris in 1826 would be an alternate history. Ward Moore did a fine parallel world in *Bring the Jubilee,* in which the United States is a rather backward nation while the Confederacy stretches all the way from Virginia to the tip of South America. Moore turned his parallel world into an alternate history at the conclusion, when his hero goes back in time to witness the Battle of Gettysburg — and changes the outcome.

More recently, William Sanders's *The Wild Blue and the Gray* is an alternate history about the Confederate Air Force fighting the Germans in World War I, with William Faulkner as the fighter pilot he never was in this world. William Gibson and Bruce Sterling staged a real tour de force a few years ago with *The Difference Engine*, about a 19th century with computers and other forms of advanced technology. The trick here is to develop the alternative worlds in plausible detail, making them exotic yet concrete and familiar.

Cyberpunk

Cyberpunk is the subgenre consisting of a near-future world of consumer electronics with huge gaps between rich and poor. William Gibson launched it with *Neuromancer* in the mid-1980s, and it's still going strong.

Cyberpunk portrays capitalism triumphant, but not very affectionately; the sympathy lies with the marginal young people trying to build lives in the waste dumps of the global economy. Unlike the utopian SF of long ago, cyberpunk authors are loudly silent about remedies for the problems they depict — which are very much the problems of today. Perhaps this reflects a passive, apolitical acceptance of injustice; more likely, cyberpunk authors pay their readers the compliment of allowing them to reach their own conclusions about social issues.

Don't worry about staying inside the boundaries of a specific genre or subgenre; the boundaries can be pretty fuzzy sometimes. For example, are parallel worlds and alternate histories subgenres of time-travel stories? Well, they can be if your characters are moving from one time line to another (as in Keith Laumer's *Worlds of the Imperium*), or creating new time lines by going into the past and changing the future (as in *Bring the Jubilee*).

But if your alternate history is set in a world where such travel doesn't happen (as in William Sanders's *Journey to Fusang*), then this particular fusion of subgenres has not occurred.

However, no subgenre is absolutely fixed. Obviously, many science fiction novels combine elements of different subgenres. Less obviously, every work in every subgenre should surprise us by exploring something so far unexpected in its conventions.

After all, the goal of both SF and fantasy is to evoke a sense of wonder by showing us something we had not expected to see, something that changes our basic vision of the world. If we try to subvert that reaction of surprise by reading only formula fiction, where everything happens the same way every time, we're really no better off than the toddler who wants the same bedtime story every night, read in exactly the same way.

So if you're going to do yet another saga about telepathic mutants living among us, find something in your story that no one's done before, not just a trivial twist (the mutants are telepathic only when their foreheads are touching) but something that makes us think about the whole idea of telepathy.

That's what I tried to do with telepathy in my first novel, *The Empire of Time:* one of the characters belongs to a tribe that's telepathic and dying out because each person literally feels everyone else's pain. Babies suffer trauma at birth because they experience their mothers' pain and that of their relatives, who feel it too. A death is equally dreadful. The point I was trying to make was that we may lack telepathy because it's better, evolutionarily, *not* to be in really close communion with others.

THE SUBGENRES OF FANTASY

Having dealt at such length with science fiction, I hope writers of fantasy will forgive me if I discuss fantasy subgenres much more briefly. Fantasy can do anything it pleases, within rather broad limits, so its divisions are less clear-cut.

Epic Fantasy

The broadest subgenre in fantasy is epic fantasy, with a whole world at stake in a gigantic battle of good against evil. The world is usually pre-industrial, with the highest technology being steel making. The political order is something like medieval European feudalism, usually in a crisis because the royal succession has been broken and the throne has been usurped. Humans share the world with various other humanoid species, and some animals have humanlike powers of thought and language. Epic fantasy easily evolves into genres like heroic fantasy and sword and sorcery.

Heroic Fantasy

The nature of the protagonist often defines subgenres of epic fantasy. In heroic fantasy, the protagonist is the legitimate heir to the throne; or the young magician who's going to put the heir on that throne, as Ged does in Le Guin's *Earthsea* trilogy; or an ordinary youth who will somehow redeem his or her society.

The protagonist has to deal with enemies who often have enormous resources; our young prince/princess/mage/redeemer has to outwit them and outmagic them, and finally outfight them, usually starting with no ally but a wise old man. Everyone in epic fantasy goes on a quest — a journey fraught with difficulties and ordeals, but absolutely essential to success. So when the prince or princess is the hero we might call this a *high quest.*

Tolkien wisely turned this high-quest convention on its head by making his hero a very ordinary person, the hobbit Frodo Baggins. Aragorn is a good companion and a fine king, but he's a bit of a stick; as the hero of *Lord of the Rings,* he would have been a disaster. Frodo and his hobbit companions give us a much better view of the stock characters, both good and evil, and it's far easier to identify with them.

A novel with an ordinary social-redeemer hero we might therefore call a *low quest* — referring to the hero's social status, but certainly not disparaging him or his worth. (When the victorious allies hail Frodo and Sam and the other hobbits, it's a great and stirring scene precisely because the human warriors recognize the hobbits as not just their equals, but their superiors.)

Heroic fantasy sometimes abandons both the princely hero and the commoner to portray a talented young magician whose power could serve good or evil depending on the choices he or she makes. Le Guin's Ged is a fine example, and one of the few such characters who grow, change, and mature. This is the subgenre of my own novels *Greenmagic* and *Redmagic,* each of which deals with the education of a young magician — male in *Greenmagic,* female in *Redmagic.* The mage-redeemer really has to look inward to find the resources to save his or her society, so the journey here is less important than the inner search; we might call this the *soul quest.*

Sword and Sorcery

Heroic fantasy shades off into sword and sorcery, where the hero relies on brute force and military skill to get him from the barbarian outback to the imperial throne. He is less a social redeemer than a social critic, whose muscle and cunning repudiate the effete niceties of civilization.

This is Conan country, and while sorcery is always important, the sword is the preferred instrument of power. Sword and sorcery is also more interested in sex than many other subgenres, and the women are often as skilled with a broadsword as the hero. L. Sprague de Camp traces this barbarian hero back to Henri Rousseau's Noble Savage, enjoying a life free of social convention; de Camp also tartly points out that real barbarians are extremely conventional, conformist types.

Sword and sorcery is traditionally set in some ancient era (Conan's Hyborian Age is some time "after the fall of Atlantis and before the rise of the sons of Aryas"), but current authors seem content to create their own wholly mythical worlds. Dave Duncan's World, in the Seventh Sword series, and Pandemia, in the Man of His Word series, are good examples.

Historical Fantasy

Some stories stay in our history but add supernatural elements, bringing us into the subgenre of historical fantasy. One example that deserves more attention than it receives is Elizabeth Marshall

Thomas's *Reindeer Moon,* set in Ice Age Siberia, whose narrator-hero dies early in the story. The narrator spends the rest of the novel as a spirit watching her kinsfolk and sometimes inhabiting other animals such as wolves and mastodons.

Modern Fantasy

Modern fantasy gives us our own world, only one in which magic operates as routinely as electricity. Sean Stewart's *Resurrection Man* is a notable example, with our modern world gradually adapting to the return of magic since about 1945. Peter S. Beagle's *A Fine and Private Place,* his first novel, is a classic of modern fantasy, set in a New York graveyard where two ghosts fall in love and a recluse converses with a wisecracking raven.

Urban Fantasy

Urban fantasy is also modern, but uses the modern metropolis as its setting — creating an entertaining contrast between magic and the grimy back alleys of downtown. Walter Jon Williams's novels *Metropolitan* and *City on Fire* are superb examples, though the second novel begins to look like science fiction.

Science Fantasy

Science fantasy blurs the borders. It offers us science so advanced that (in Sir Arthur C. Clarke's memorable phrase) it's indistinguishable from magic. Or it gives us magic operating as advanced science might in our world, propelling spacecraft or transmitting energy. The British writer Peter Dickinson created a great example in *The Blue Hawk,* set in a decaying Egypt-like civilization ruled by invisible but detectable gods; at the end, Dickinson brings in enough of a scientific explanation to make it science fantasy rather than heroic fantasy. I tried to do something similar in *Eyas,* which for most of its length reads like low-quest heroic fantasy and then shifts into science fiction.

Is that fair to do to your readers, who may have wanted a straight fantasy anyway? Maybe not, though the ending of any story tries to make readers see events in a different light. In my case, I was trying to create a world full of fantasy-style wonders, and then to suggest that reality could be full of wonders after all.

The Enchanted Grove

The enchanted grove is what you might call the subgenre that transports our hero from this world to one of fantasy. Le Guin's young-adult novel *The Beginning Place* is a very good example. Here we have a special place where a gateway between worlds appears — usually in a setting of untouched nature.

Religious Fantasy

Religious fantasy may be highly allegorical, like C. S. Lewis's Narnia novels, or it may treat religious themes with flat-footed realism, like James Blish's *Black Easter,* where Satan and all his devils deceive humans into opening a gateway from Hell to Earth. A variant of religious fantasy uses the gods of Greek or Norse mythology, or of other cultures, as characters. Neil Gaiman's *Anansi Boys* is an excellent example of the use of African gods in a modern/urban fantasy setting.

Parody

With so many authors working in so many genres, parody is never far away. Northrop Frye argues that literature is "displaced" myth: we used to tell stories about gods and semidivine humans but now we tell them about ordinary people (even about people less intelligent or free than ourselves). The effect, at least at first, is one of parody, of poking fun at the king by putting his robes on a swineherd (who also looks pretty funny in those robes). When we drag the transcendent into our own tedious, grubby little world, it can seem very silly. Terry Pratchett has made himself a rich man by pointing this out, over and over again, in his Discworld novels.

To the extent that parody short-circuits our stock responses and makes us think about what we're reading, it's extremely useful. But a really skillful parodist may give us what seems like the straight goods, with just enough of a twist to make our stock responses a tiny bit uncomfortable. Such a parodist is far more subversive than the slapstick author who brings in thick-skulled pseudo-Conans and Gandalfs with senile dementia.

FANTASY CLICHES

The Grand List of Fantasy Cliches:
www.geocities.com/Area51/Labyrinth/8584/stuff/
cliche.html

The Not-So-Grand List of Overused Fantasy Cliches:
http://amethyst-angel.com/cliche.html

The Fantasy Novelist's Exam:
www.rinkworks.com/fnovel/

Slipstream

This is a kind of catch-all term, proposed by Bruce Sterling in 1989 and gradually finding acceptance. It's "slipstream" because it's not mainstream, but it slips through the cracks in "normal" SF and fantasy categories. The author may give us a familiar, ordinary kind of world in which nevertheless very strange things happen.

John Updike's *Toward the End of Time* is a good example: a year in the life of a retired financial adviser in 2020 Massachusetts, after a disastrous U.S.-China nuclear war. It might seem like ordinary SF, except that some passages are simply … weird. A gigantic toroidal spaceship appears near Earth, orbits for a while, and then vanishes; living machines, spontaneously generated in junkheaps, are crawling about in the woods. Either element could have been the core of an ordinary SF story. But here they're just events in the narrator's life, like his gardening or his prostate cancer.

Other mainstream writers have explored the freedom of slipstream: Gore Vidal in *The Smithsonian Institution* and *Live from Golgotha,* Margaret Atwood in *The Handmaid's Tale,* Thomas Pynchon in *V* and almost everything else he's written.

Slipstream isn't just Latin American magic realism with a non-Latin American accent. It's a way of using SF and fantasy conventions to evoke a world in which, as Sterling puts it, "nothing we know makes 'a lot of sense,' and perhaps even that nothing ever could." If that strikes a chord with you, I suggest you read extensively in the field and draw your own generalizations about its significant conventions. In a subgenre so new, that could be either a very short list or a very long one!

As we've seen in looking at the subgenres of science fiction and fantasy, the obsession with power demands an underlying theme: Be careful what you wish for, because you may get it. To do justice to that theme, you need to remember the devastating judgment of the Hainishman on the Earthmen who have caused a terrible mess in Le Guin's novella *The Word for World Is Forest*. After hearing their defensive, self-serving arguments, the Hainishman says simply: "You have not thought things through."

Whatever genre you write in, don't let that judgment apply to you.

WRITING FOR YOUNG ADULTS AND CHILDREN

Most of the subgenres I've discussed are also the subgenres for young readers. The difference in a young adult (YA) story is chiefly the age of the main characters. The protagonist in a YA science fiction or fantasy story is usually a young person, often in early adolescence and just as often uncertain of his or her place in society. Moral issues are more urgent and personal than in many "adult" tales; if YA protagonists make the wrong moral decisions, they compromise their own adult identities as well as the security of the society they wish to live in.

The protagonist may start by rejecting adult authority (or by being rejected). But the authority of the very old, or the very strange, often provides essential guidance. Literature since the Greeks has been full of alliances between the old and the young against the middle-aged clods who are running things, so we can expect them in YA science fiction and fantasy.

The old person is often a mentor, such as Obi-Wan Kenobi in *Star Wars,* who recognizes and calls forth some crucial talent in the protagonist. In other cases the estranged young person makes an alliance with some other outsider, often literally an alien like E.T.

At some point, however, the protagonist must fly solo. The mentor is dead or unavailable, and some ordeal looms; the protagonist undergoes it alone. This rite of passage leads to adult status, but it is also a kind of death and rebirth (see Chapter 13 on symbolism for more about this transition). The child is no more; the adult, however, is still very new in his or her role.

The task for writers of YA fiction is to deal effectively with serious issues — love, death, loyalty, betrayal, courage, cowardice — in terms that young readers will understand and respond to. Kurt Vonnegut observes that only teenagers and SF writers think about Big Issues like the meaning of life and the fate of the universe; the rest of us are too busy saving for retirement and fighting traffic to reflect on those issues.

The YA author also has to consider adult anxieties, since adults buy most books for children and many for teenagers — so YA books often have to steer away from sensational topics or controversial politics.

Sometimes such avoidance is actually good craft. A long, explicit sex scene might make a YA fantasy novel very popular with 11- and 12-year-olds, but it will surely derail the story, which ought to be about more than inducing pubescent palpitations. It's also likely to be bad business: in the unlikely event that you could get the scene past your editor, schools and libraries would surely avoid buying your book.

The language of a YA story should not be dumbed down by adult standards. Robert Heinlein (the Obi-Wan Kenobi to generations of us speculative writers) used to say that he kept the language in his adult novels as simple as possible — but in his novels for kids, he threw in big words that kids would enjoy wrestling with. Listen to the master!

The subtext of any YA story is that learning not only solves problems but is a pleasure in itself. Over half a century ago, in Heinlein's *Space Cadet,* I read that members of the Space Force would be studying even on the day they retired. I have not forgotten this, and neither have hundreds of thousands of other young readers who have kept learning as they have grown older.

This is not to say you should write dense, complex prose. Use your word processor's grammar checker to determine your story's reading level. The longer your sentences, and the more polysyllables per sentence, the higher the grade level needed to understand your text. Unless a rich, ornate style is essential to the tale you're telling, you should be able to keep your reading level at grade five or six and still offer a challenging story. In the science fiction novel I've been working on lately, the reading level is grade five. I'd worry if it started rising. (See Chapter 14 for more about readability scales.)

4

Creating Your Fictional World

When I was 12 years old or so, I read a story about a boy who'd created a world with a map — a world so real that, when another boy gave him a hard time, monsters came out of a swamp on the map and disposed of the bully.

The idea knocked me out. At once I was lost in imaginative cartography, mapping lost kingdoms and assigning them to myself and my friends. (Maybe I was already predisposed to this love of imaginary worlds by living in Mexico City — which had plenty of maps and painted landscapes of the lost and destroyed city of Tenochtitlán, gleaming on the shores of a vanished lake.) The hardcover Conan books of the mid-1950s also had maps of "Hyborian Age" Europe, which looked much more interesting than its modern version. When the first volume of *The Lord of the Rings* came out, the foldout map in the back was worth the price of the whole book.

Happily plagiarizing both Robert E. Howard and J. R. R. Tolkien, I concocted a map with the good guys in the northwest and the bad guys in the southeast, and wrote a 25,000-word novella in which my friends, under thinly disguised names, battled evil across my imaginary continent.

Obviously I wasn't alone. Countless science fiction and fantasy writers have created their own worlds, some of which have become more real to readers than the other planets in the solar system. Arrakis, Middle Earth, Winter, the strange America of Terry Bisson's *Talking Man* — these worlds are as vivid as Marcel Proust's Paris or Joseph Conrad's central Africa.

The creation of SF worlds in particular has become a specialized craft, with any number of technical demands: you have to locate your world the right distance from the kind of star you've specified, you have to give it a suitable rotation period and year, your biosphere has to produce the right mix of atmospheric gases and a suitable climate. If that sounds daunting, you can even find technical consultants on the Web who will, for a price, design a world for you.

Fantasy is a little more relaxed, but all too often the fantasy author just changes the place names and coastlines of Middle Earth. So we get yet another geography of randomly distributed mountains and deserts, lots of forests, picturesque chains of islands, and names that seem to have come from a Fantasy Name Generator application.

Well, the techie stuff about planetary details is a useful exercise, and it might give you good ideas for the story you're placing on your world. But the writer of science fiction or fantasy must keep answering one simple question: *Why?*

Why set your story on the surface of a neutron star or on a radiation-soaked rock in the galactic center? Why send your hero questing through a temperate-zone forest, or a frozen tundra, or any other particular kind of geography?

One simple answer is that you're writing a kind of "thought experiment": if life could exist on a neutron star, what would it be like, and how would it behave, given what we know about the physics of neutron stars? The story's appeal therefore comes from instructing and entertaining readers at the same time.

For fantasy writers, the answer is that the setting is traditional, or simply convenient. (My own fantasy novels are set in a kind of parallel-world North America, with most of the action taking place in the mountains and prairies of west central Alberta — spectacular country that I happen to know very well, so I didn't have to make much up.)

DEMONIC WORLDS AND PARADISE WORLDS

Bear in mind that literature gives us a chance to create two different kinds of world: the *demonic world* where everything is hostile to human needs and desires, and the *paradise world* where everything serves and supports those needs and desires. Typically, the fantasy story begins in a paradise, though it may be an ironic one. At any rate, it's some kind of stable society.

Once the action of your tale is under way, however, your characters are exiled from paradise and struggling in the grip of the demonic: the Black Riders are in the Shire, every corner of Middle Earth holds a real or potential threat, and the enemy will haunt the hobbits' minds until they destroy the One Ring and regain paradise.

I suggest that you start with some kind of symbolic reason for the kind of world you want, whether in science fiction or fantasy — a world that is symbolically a paradise, changed to (or at least threatened by) a demonic world.

Ursula K. Le Guin does this beautifully. In *The Left Hand of Darkness,* the planet of androgynous humans is in an ice age, and the natives call it Winter. Only in the brief, fierce summers does the snow melt. This reflects the cycle of "kemmer," in which people are essentially sexless for four-fifths of the time, and then completely concerned with sex for the remaining fifth. And in *The Dispossessed,* her anarchist society lives on Anarres, a dry, infertile moon orbiting the rich, decadently capitalistic home world of Urras. The anarchists' dreams have been infertile also, and their society is slowly dying. So is Urras, but more dramatically.

Think also about some of the geographical conventions of science fiction — especially the womblike world, closed off from the outside. Maybe your world should be similarly womblike: an isolated valley like Shangri-La, an interstellar generation ship, a research station on a hostile planet. You may even create such a symbolic setting without even thinking about it — as I did with "New Shackleton Station" in *Icequake,* an Antarctic research base buried in the Ross Ice Shelf. In *Eyas* I consciously created a uterine world, the Gulf of Islands — an inland sea with only one major outlet to the ocean, through which a violent tide surges twice a day. The Gulf of Islands is a paradise of naked people living more or less happily until invaders overwhelm it; thereafter Eyas, the hero, must face a hostile demonic world and must try to conquer it to regain his lost paradise.

The hero, if an inquisitive outsider, often enters this womblike paradise through a kind of symbolic death — a departure from the larger world outside — and then goes through a symbolic rebirth on leaving it again (not always willingly!).

A SENSE OF WHAT IS NATURAL

If your heart is set on writing about a neutron star and the creatures that inhabit it, one symbolic message will be inescapable: that intelligent beings will arise everywhere in the universe, and that whatever their form or setting, their behavior will be understandable to us, and ours to them.

In his novel *Iceworld,* for example, Hal Clement gives us a race that lives in a high-temperature environment where sulfur is a liquid. Yet these beings are susceptible to addiction, and especially to tobacco from Earth (the "iceworld" of the title). No matter how bizarre your aliens or demons, they will ultimately be much like us; otherwise we wouldn't be interested in them.

A simple-minded approach to this underlying premise is to

make the aliens exactly like us, only with pointy ears or corrugated foreheads. But on a more sophisticated level, the vision of a humanly comprehensible universe is rich with possibilities. If life on a neutron star behaves like us, then we might well look at our own environment, which we usually ignore as fish do water, and see it with renewed wonder and perception. All science assumes the universe is knowable; your neutron star's creatures, by being themselves knowable, affirm a deep-rooted human faith.

By all means have fun with the technical details of the world you create: the physiological effects of a planet with 0.8 Earth gravity, the influence of multiple moons that sometimes create extra-high tides, washing creatures into one another's marine ecosystems.

But remember that you're not creating curiosities; you're trying to evoke in your readers a wider, deeper sense of what is *natural,* not just what is weird or bizarre. The lilacs in your garden and the aliens on your neutron star are all part of a single, comprehensible universe.

The same is true of fantasy worlds. You may have more freedom to set the rules of such worlds, but they must make some kind of sense in human terms. And once you set your rules, you have to abide by them. If your characters must deal with the supernatural, it is natural to them: a goblin is as real as a dog, and a spell has effects as observable as a viral infection.

I got a crash course in this principle when I started writing *Greenmagic.* My hero's mother, Tilcalli, is a highly talented young witch who is prepared to use some powerful spells to achieve her ends. But I realized almost at once that if she could just throw spells the way cowboys throw lariats, I had no story. Tilcalli needed to be talented, but even her talent needed limits.

So I made it a rule of magic that it would work on material objects like plants, or on the weather, or by creating powerful illusions — but to cast a spell on a human mind would be dangerous and close to impossible. And that's the kind of spell Tilcalli casts on Prince Albohar to make him fall in love with her and protect her while her son learns both his mother's magic and that of Albohar's people, the Badakhar. This helped me demonstrate Tilcalli's talent and still gave me room to tell a story.

I made it another principle that exercising magic would exhaust the magician — the bigger the spell, the longer the resulting inability to use magic. So magicians use their powers frugally, and when Tilcalli's son begins to acquire magical skill, he scares everyone because he doesn't get tired.

Maybe you want a world in which the magician energizes his or her spells with human blood, as I did in *Redmagic;* having made that decision, you have to work out the implications and live within the limits they set. My villains, related to the Aztecs, are the Exteca — "Blood people." My Exteca sorcerers' human sacrifices brought a prosperity that has to be sustained with yet more sacrifices, forcing their culture into endless expansion and conquest like a pyramid marketing scheme. And since these charming people are related to the Aztecs in our world, they build their temples as pyramids.

PARALLEL WORLDS

My Exteca bring up a sore subject: the relationship of your fantasy world to ours. While I didn't explain it in so many words, the world of *Greenmagic* and *Redmagic* is geographically identical to ours. But it's in some kind of parallel world where magic works, and which a divine being has rather arbitrarily colonized with small groups of various pre-industrial cultures from our world.

So a Stone Age Irish culture is thriving in the San Francisco Bay area, while the Exteca are expanding rapidly from their base in Los Angeles. The warlike, nomadic Badakhar are a branch of the original Indo-Europeans, speaking a language close to Proto-Indo-European. (It turned out to be a good language for villains, full of hawking and spitting.) They've conquered the Cantareans, agricultural American Indians who had been living peacefully on the Alberta prairies; a few have retreated into the Rocky Mountains around Jasper. Farther west live the dragons, intelligent dinosaurs who have no language as we know it but who are masters of their own kind of magic.

I created this parallel world because I wanted some kind of connection to our own world, and characters who would seem familiar to readers.

FANTASY WORLDS

You can certainly create a fantasy world from scratch, with humans living in a world entirely their own, making a living in a different ecosystem, and creating cultures unrelated to any that we on Earth have devised.

If you do so, however, you'll have to stamp out any and all echoes of our world. You can't have one character with a synthetic name like Glanchki, and another named Christopher. If your characters are contending with real live gods, those divinities better not have names like Kwannon or Loki or Yahweh ... unless you want to suggest that our gods are superintending other universes as well.

By the same token, social titles and institutions should be very different from ours. If you give us kings and knights and earls and peasants, all running around conquering empires and invading dukedoms, you've missed the point. Granted, you might "translate" from the original terms into those more familiar to your readers, as Tolkien does in *The Lord of the Rings,* but that might ruin the very strangeness you've set out to create.

You have a couple of alternatives for this aspect of fantasy-world creation. First, you could put everything into English, as I did in *Eyas.* The villages had English names like Longstrand and Rainfalling; the people had names like Brightspear and Silken. (Eyas is an Old English name for a baby hawk.) I pushed this farther than I should have, so that even terms in the languages of other species, like centaurs and lotors, came out as English.

Second, you could create at least the rudiments of an artificial language, with a reasonably extensive vocabulary and a basic grammar. If it's fairly consistent in its sounds and structure, you can then build personal and place names out of it, as well as terms for social rank and institution. In *Greenmagic* I had a Badakh ruler, Albohar, from the Proto-Indo-European words for "white hair." His title, Aryo, comes from the Proto-Indo-European word for "king" or "leader." Albohar is indeed the fair-haired boy at first, though he changes as he grows older. (The echo of "Aryan" in the highly racist Badakhar gave their culture a sour tang of Iron Age Nazism.)

So even if your names are made up, they can still mean something, as our own names and titles do. *Lord* comes from Old English for "loaf guard," or protector of the community food supplies. *Lady* in Old English means "peace weaver." Your artificial titles and names can be equally evocative.

In fantasy we used to be free to ignore workaday details and to concentrate on the fun. Traditional fantasy worlds seemed populated strictly by royalty, wizards, evil aristocrats, bandits, and loyal retainers. No one had to work for a living, the king never had to meet a payroll, and the retainers never went on strike.

Even as recently as Tolkien, we have little sense of people engaging in manufacturing, agriculture, or trade except for stuff like "pipeweed." Yet the hobbits enjoy a dull suburban prosperity, briefly threatened by Saruman's failed attempt to introduce industrialism. It's as if Tolkien were deliberately rejecting the whole crass idea of making a living in the Shire.

Since then, however, fantasy worlds have generally grown more realistic. Nations live by trade or industrial production; magicians are as functional as plumbers or computer programmers. In Walter Jon Williams's urban fantasies, mages handle plasm like electrical engineers running power stations. In part, this new realism is a kind of ironic comment on, even a parody of, earlier fantasy; it's not much of a step from Williams's plasm to Terry Pratchett's octarine and all the pratfalls of Discworld.

But beneath the parody is a genuine and commendable purpose: to make magic seem more real, and therefore more wonderful, more awe-inspiring. When Le Guin's Ged is still a little boy named Duny, he lives in a rustic backwater where people really do make livings, farming or herding goats or working as bronzesmiths as Duny's father does. His first displays of talent seem all the more vivid and astonishing because his world is so matter-of-fact. However you organize your fantasy world, then, make it as gritty and real and ordinary as you can; the more ordinary it is, even in its marvels, the more marvelous your readers will find it.

Part 2:
The Craft of
Writing Science Fiction
and Fantasy

5

Developing Efficient Work Habits

Different writers face different advantages and drawbacks in forming good writing habits. The circumstances of your personal life may make it easy or hard to find writing time, but time itself is not the real issue — it's habit. Writing must be something you do regularly, like brushing your teeth. The writer who waits for inspiration will wait even longer for a complete, published short story or novel.

Writing habits flourish best in routine, but the efficient writer also exploits opportunity.

ROUTINE

Set aside some time every day when you can work undisturbed for an hour or two — first thing in the morning, during lunch, after dinner, whenever you can set aside other demands. Try to find a writing time when few people phone or visit. Ideally, your writing time will be the same time of day each day. Your family and friends will soon build their routines around yours. With luck, they will resent your unscheduled appearances during your writing time, and will send you packing back to your desk.

Keep your writing equipment (paper, pens, software manuals, etc.) in your writing place, close at hand. Minimize distractions like interesting new magazines and books. If a cup of coffee and some background music make you feel less lonely, by all means enjoy them.

Use the time you spend doing household chores as thinking time: a chance to review what you've written so far and to consider where your writing should go next. Walking the dog or vacuuming the carpet can provide more ideas than you expect.

This is really just controlled daydreaming, letting your mind freewheel in a particular direction: what the heroine should do in the next chapter, how the hero would respond to being abandoned in a bombed-out space station, how the villain developed his evil character. But the process doesn't seem to work if you just sit and stare at the wall. You need to be up and moving in some automatic pattern.

Keep a Writing Journal

Don't lean on others for editorial advice and encouragement — least of all people you're emotionally involved with. Spouses, friends, and roommates rarely have both editorial perceptiveness and the tact to express it without infuriating you or breaking your heart. Empty praise will get you nowhere; unconstructive criticism can destroy your novel in an instant. This is especially true if your significant other just doesn't enjoy the genre you're writing in. If your boyfriend likes hard SF and laughs at your obsession with dragons, he's the last person to ask for criticism.

Instead, *be your own editor:* set aside regular times to write yourself letters discussing your own work, articulating what's good and less good in it. In the process you'll easily solve problems that could otherwise grow into full-blown writer's block. On a computer, the letters can form a continuous journal, recording your reactions to the evolving work. Checking back to the first journal entries can help keep you on track — or dramatically show you how far you've moved from your original concept.

Writing a letter to yourself is especially helpful if you're beginning to have anxieties about the story. Sometimes we try to suppress those anxieties, which only makes them worse. Anxiety turns to frustration and despair, and finally we abandon the whole project. If you can actually write down what bothers you about your heroine, or your plot, or whatever, the answer to the problem often suggests itself. The act of turning our chaotic thoughts into orderly sentences seems to lead to much quicker and more satisfying solutions.

Keep a Daily Log

In addition to these self-addressed letters, keep a daily log of your progress. Word processors with word-count functions are powerful encouragers. The log can give you a sense of accomplishment, especially on big projects, and can enable you to set realistic completion deadlines. For example, if you know you can write 500 words in an hour, and you write three hours a week, you can have a completed novel manuscript of 75,000 words in 50 weeks. If you write ten hours a week, the manuscript will be complete in 15 weeks.

Keep a Project "Bible"

A project "bible" is a list of facts, names, and so on that you expect to be using for constant reference, and it's especially important in SF and fantasy because you're creating a world full of special details. If you have some important research findings you plan to use, put them in the bible along with their sources.

Include lists of characters' names (with descriptions, so their eyes don't change color) and unusual words or spellings.

If you don't have a laptop, the best format for this bible may be a binder, big enough to hold standard loose-leaf filler paper, which you can carry with you. (A word of caution: if your bible gets too big to carry easily, you're defeating one of its purposes. It should be available whenever and wherever, so if need be you can work in your dentist's waiting room or on the bus.)

USING DEAD TIME CONSTRUCTIVELY

If you decide you can't write unless you're seated at your computer with Mozart on the stereo and no one else in the house, you're just making life harder for yourself. Your day-to-day routine will always contain dead time — periods when you're away from home (or at least away from your workplace) with no other task at hand. You might be waiting in a doctor's office, on a bus, or trapped in a large, dull meeting. If you're writing SF or fantasy, chances are it's because you're already a highly skilled daydreamer who can drift off to other worlds without much trouble.

So use that dead time constructively by carrying your project bible in which you can record at least a few lines of whatever you're daydreaming about. Or you might jot down some background notes about your project, or a self-editing idea that's just occurred to you. You can then use these when you're back at your desk producing finished text.

These are general habits that will help you at all stages of the process of writing a short story or novel. But you may also find that you need to understand those stages and adapt your habits to each

Here's a slightly outrageous tip: Don't respect the text. Just because you've written something down doesn't mean it has a right to exist. If your internal editor can find a better way to say something, junk the original version and go with the new one. If you can't find a better way, and the passage really isn't good, junk it.

Outrageous tip number two: Not enough hours in the day for everything you have to do? Stop watching television.

of them. You may not do yourself any good if you plunge into the writing phase before you've decided just what kind of story you want to tell, and why.

HOW DO YOU GET IDEAS?

Here you are, trying to write in a genre based on ideas, and you can't think of anything! Or at least, anything that hasn't been done to death already. Don't be discouraged. An editor, after I'd pitched him on a new novel, replied: "Well, it's not wildly original."

"Would you buy it if it really were wildly original?" I asked.

"Probably not," he admitted.

New ideas come along so rarely that we're still reeling from those that Darwin and Einstein came up with. If you can find intriguing variations on an old idea, you'll do well. Here are some suggestions.

Group Brainstorming

Kick around story ideas with a friend or colleague and see what variations emerge. Just remember never to reject a suggestion; instead say: "Yeah, or …" and you'll keep the ideas flowing.

Solo Brainstorming

Write yourself a letter, discussing your current ideas (or lack thereof), and you'll be amazed to see some real surprises coming out of the basement of your subconscious, where your writer lives.

Reading and Reacting

You should be routinely reading several science journals, popular or otherwise, looking for discoveries and debates. In addition, you should be reading and taking notes on as many books about science and scientists as you can manage. (If you're writing fantasy, a grounding in science won't hurt, and both SF and fantasy writers should be reading folklore, anthropology, and history as well.)

Even newspapers can inspire good ideas. I first ran across the theory of Antarctic ice-sheet surges in a short newspaper story. A little research unearthed the original scientific paper, and I was soon embarked on *Icequake* — which ultimately sold 200,000 copies.

You should also be reading both good and bad work in your chosen genre. The junk will warn you away from bad practices, and encourage you at the same time: if these bozos can get into print, surely you can! If you think the good writers are impossibly superior to you, write short reviews of their work, for your eyes only, discussing what they do well. Chances are you'll find you can put your finger on specific techniques once you start talking about them. And once you see the technique, you can start using it too.

Anthropologizing

Look at the dress, behavior, and language of members of some particular group. Why do they do the things they do, and what might they be doing in fifty years?

Extrapolating

Ask yourself, If this goes on, where does it take us? For example, the U.S. Census Bureau predicts that in 2050 the American population will total 419 million, of whom 13 million women and 8 million men will be aged 85 or older. That is, 21 million people born before 1966 will still be alive at midcentury. Some will even remember the end of World War II.

What kind of society will it be when almost one citizen in 20 is pushing 100? And what will young people think of all those old folks?

Or look at it in more personal terms: What will it be like to be one of 13 million very old women, almost all of whom have long since lost their husbands? Could we see a kind of sorority form, women caring for other women? And what about the men?

6

Research and Soul Search

One of the great, underrated pleasures of writing fiction is how much you learn in the process.

You are, after all, trying to tell a highly plausible lie. Even if your story is about people still unborn, on planets not yet discovered, we want to believe it. Your readers' eagerness to be deceived is a great gift to you, and you shouldn't abuse it! That means giving them as much truth as possible — solid facts, reasonable conjecture, sound extrapolation — so your whoppers sound believable too.

An old writing-class maxim is that you should "write what you know about." But that doesn't mean you're limited to stories about life in your particular neighborhood; it just means you have to learn as much as possible about your subject.

Case in point: A few years ago I was writing *Rogue Emperor,* a time-travel novel set in Rome in the year AD 100. When I started, I thought I knew a lot about ancient Rome; a little research soon taught me the scope of my ignorance, so I began reading voraciously. It was no hardship — it was like a detective's hunt for critical clues. I was searching for little details that would make imperial Rome come alive, make it feel as crowded and concrete as downtown Mexico City.

I learned that dead gladiators were temporarily stowed in a chamber under the seats of the Colosseum, and if they had no friends to bury them, their corpses went into a pit not far away. I learned that women were sometimes gladiators (technically, they were gladiatrices). And that gave me enough for a critical scene in the first chapter, when my hero, Jerry Pierce, encounters a gladiatrix in that chamber, weeping over the corpse of her lover. He offers her the simple consolation of a hand on her shoulder, and thereby saves his own life ... because later he will need her cooperation when he himself is thrown into the arena against professional gladiators.

Sometimes your research will offer up these details and you just have to go with them. In other cases, the story itself demands that you go back and dig up something. In the middle of *Rogue Emperor,* Jerry Pierce is trying to cross Rome in the dead of night to reach the home of Pliny the Younger, one of the consuls administering the empire on behalf of the emperor. I knew from my research that all-night wine shops were popular hangouts, so I sent Pierce into one in search of a guide. Who should be sitting in this particular dive but the famous poet Juvenal, exceedingly drunk.

Well, I hadn't counted on meeting a celebrity; all I knew about Juvenal was that he was a poet of the period. Period. So I had to scamper off to the library to read his verses and learn about his life. He turned out to be a bit of a jerk: reactionary, snobbish, xenophobic. Didn't matter. He knew how to get to Pliny's house, and a lot more. I was glad to have made his acquaintance.

So why was Pierce looking for Pliny the Younger? Because my research showed that in the year 100, Pliny was consul. This was a historical fact. If I wanted to stay in AD 100, and to write about Roman political issues of that year, then I would have to deal with him. It was also a very convenient fact, because Pliny wrote a lot, and many of his letters have survived, so I learned many details about his life and society.

Pliny was a necessity. Juvenal was a windfall, something my subconscious dropped into my lap. Your research should enable you to deal with both necessities and surprises.

LIBRARY RESEARCH

Your first research destination is your local public library. You'll find plenty of books on almost any topic, enough to give you a rough familiarity with almost any subject that your story is going to deal with. But I suggest you use them in a slightly unusual way.

First, bring your project bible with you. You've been using it to write notes to yourself, to file your character résumés, and so on; now it's going to start containing detailed research.

You begin with the library's index. You go to a particular subject — let's say it's Babylonian mythology, which you've decided is more interesting for your fantasy novel than the boring old Greeks and Norse. You find two or three titles. For each one, you write down the title, author, publisher, and date of publication on a separate sheet of paper, along with the book's library call number.

Then you go to the shelves and track them down. Chances are that at least some of your sources will be in the reference section and don't circulate outside the library. You may be able to photocopy some sections, but for now you're just going to scan these sources with your pen and paper at hand.

What's more, you're going to scan them *backward* — by starting with the index and bibliography. The index will point you straight to key topics like the Babylonian pantheon, creation myths, and so on. Instead of plowing through page after page, you just learn what you need. (Of course you're going to stumble into unexpected good information as well.) You take notes on key facts: names of gods, attributes, relationships to other gods.

In some cases, a quick scan of the index and relevant passages will show that this source, at least, is useless. At least you've learned this in a hurry; on the page where you've given the book's title and author, you write down "Useless." That way, if the book turns up later in some other index, and you've forgotten about it, you won't waste time tracking it down again.

Let's assume you've found a really good source on Babylonian mythology. After scanning the most interesting passages, you go to the bibliography. Here, in a few convenient pages, you have most of the key books and journal articles on your subject. Many won't be in your local library, but some nearby university may have them — or they may be available through interlibrary loan.

Public libraries have their limits. If you can get access to a local university library, you'll be in much better shape. This is especially true if you're looking for very recent technical or scientific information; a big university library will carry journals and books that no public library will. But many public libraries can arrange interlibrary loans with colleges and universities.

Inevitably you also explore Babylonian history, politics, social structure, and technology; you learn not only about Babylon but also its neighbors and enemies. Everything gives you possible ideas for your story. You see intriguing parallels with modern life and myth, as well as startling divergences. (My research into ancient Rome taught me that it was a lot like the Mexico City I'd grown up in — even in the design of apartment buildings and in ceremonies like bullfights.)

As you absorb all this, you're taking notes and also starting to write letters to yourself about what you're learning. Could this particular god serve as a villain? Does this particular king remind you of your story's hero?

Maybe your subconscious wanted Babylonian myth for no particular reason, but it's learning, too. Perhaps the original pattern of your story, formed when you knew little about Babylon, is changing, becoming more Babylonian and less Western. This could be a great advantage, or a serious problem. After all, no ancient Babylonians will read your novel, and modern readers may be baffled by some of your imagery and events. They just won't have the cultural references to make sense of them. (I learned this the hard way, trying to teach a Hemingway short story to a class of college students in China. The story was full of references that meant nothing to my students, so I had to walk them through it, explaining mysteries like why an American town would have a Greek restaurant.)

RESEARCH ON THE INTERNET

The Internet now makes research much easier, of course. For one thing, you can usually explore the catalogs of university libraries all over the world, and in some cases arrange either a loan of materials or a straight download from the net.

The explosion of the World Wide Web is an especially welcome event. With Google and a little practice, you can track down material in seconds. Your problem may well be information overload — so much stuff you won't know what to do with it all.

Here's an example: After writing the previous two sentences, I went on the Web and logged in to Google Advanced Search. I typed in *Babylonian mythology*. In one-fifth of a second I learned that Google had found 29,700 items matching my phrase. (In 1997 when I did the same exercise, the Alta Vista search engine found 354 hits.) The very first Google hit was "The Assyro-Babylonian Mythology FAQ." The FAQ (frequently asked questions) had several sections, including information on "older gods" and younger ones named Annunaki and Igigi. Great stuff, I thought.

Then I found a section referring to Cthulhu, a deity created by H. P. Lovecraft that he attributed to Babylon, and another section referring to the goddess Tiamat as a character in Advanced Dungeons and Dragons, the role-playing game. Well, I thought, maybe Babylonian mythology isn't quite the virgin territory I'd imagined! But I'd already learned a lot with just a few clicks of my mouse. The third item was the Wikipedia entry on Babylonian mythology, which had even more information and over two dozen links to further resources.

TIPS ON WEB RESEARCH USING GOOGLE

When I wrote the first edition of this book in the late 1990s, I had to assume that some readers would be total innocents about the World Wide Web, so I explained how to set a browser's preferences to make pages more readable. I also assumed that people would prefer this or that search engine. Since then, Google has crowded most other search engines right out of the picture.

But you may not be using Google to its maximum potential, so here are some suggestions. These suggestions are based on Google's own search advice.

- Set your **Preferences**: Choose English as your interface language; select "search for pages in any language"; under "number of results," select 50 or 100 results per page; and choose to open results in a new browser window. And then click to "save preferences."

- From Google's home page (www.google.com), click on **Advanced Search** (www.google.com/advance_ search?hl=en). Bookmark this page, or better yet, drag it to your desktop or browser toolbar. This is a good place to start from.

- Use the **exact phrase** field to find word strings, for example, *Canadian freelance writing, extrasolar planets, buckyballs in nanotechnology*. No quotation marks are needed. (Quotation marks *are* needed, however, if you aren't using this Advanced Search page.)

- Use the **all of the words** field in addition to "exact phrase" to add other words related to your search. Example: Exact phrase *extrasolar planets* with all the words *gas giants*. Or use **without the words** to exclude terms from the search. Example: Exact phrase *Canadian freelance writer* without the words *journalism nonfiction*.

- Right under the search fields, there are a number of other ways to narrow down your search: Specify the **language** of the resulting web pages, the **file format** (Word, Excel,

PDF, etc.), the time the web page was **last updated**, the **location of your search terms** in the page (text, title, links, etc.), the **domain name** (i.e., searching only within one specific website), the **usage rights** of your results, and whether your results will be **filtered or unfiltered.**

- If you scroll down to the **Page-Specific Search**, you can find pages similar to a page whose URL you know, or find pages that link to a particular URL. See what happens when you type *http://crofsblogs.typepad.com/fiction/* into either of these fields.

- The Topic-Specific Searches include links to **other Google databases.** (The topics of Apple Macintosh, BSD Unix, Linux, and Microsoft will probably be irrelevant to your web research!) Google is uploading more and more books to its Google Book Search as well as more scholarly papers to its Google Scholar.

There are other ways to narrow down your search results by typing specific words and symbols within the search field. This can either be in the "all of the words" field, or the field that comes up if you aren't using Advanced Search.

- Search for synonyms and related words: Put a tilde (~) before the term: *~H5N1*

- Find web pages with a definition: Type *define:magma*

- Find a flexible phrase: Put an asterisk as a substitute for any word in a phrase: *Capilano **

- Search for a page that no longer exists: Click on <u>Cached</u> under any result on the results page that doesn't seem to work, or type *cache:www.lostsite.com* (the URL of the site you're searching for). Google may still have it cached somewhere.

- Search within a specific website or domain: Type *"avian flu" site:www.guardian.co.uk*

- Specify what is in the URL of the resulting web pages: Type *"life expectancy" inurl:gov*. This will come up with all the government websites that contain that phrase.

- Search web page titles: Type *Capilano intitle:student loans*

- Search number ranges, which includes anything from years to prices: Type *1880..1895 "Canada's prime ministers"*, or *camera $500..750*

For more Google Web search features, check out www.google.com/intl/en/help/features.html.

Downloading Information

Once you've found a source, what do you do with all the information it contains? You could read it off the screen and take notes, but that's the hard way. I suggest you save any useful page to your hard drive, since there is always the chance that the page will be taken down from the Web, or that the URL changes. Your browser should have a button or menu command that lets you do this, and gives you the chance to name the page yourself while selecting the place where you want to save it.

You can rapidly save a number of pages this way, and then go back later and open them up using either your web browser again, or your word processor. Web pages can be saved as HTML files (if given the option, save without the pictures and exact formatting or you will have a jumble of files on your hard drive), or as straight text files without formatting. If the web page is a PDF, you can also download it as a fully formatted file that you read with a tool called Adobe Acrobat Reader. Note that if you do open up an HTML or text file in your word processor, you can change the font, point size, and layout to whatever you like.

But you can also print straight from the screen. If you do so, be sure you've set your type display small enough to fit the text on regular size paper. The typefaces Georgia or Times New Roman at 14 points can be awkwardly big for printing; a table, for example, may be too big to print without losing text on the margins. So go back to your options menu and reset the point size to 9 or 10, or adjust the zoom in print preview. Then you can print out and be sure to get everything.

You may also want to organize some sites in your browser by creating a folder of bookmarks (also called "favorites"). For example, you could create a folder titled Babylonian Gods and then save the URLs of the best sites you discover through your Google search.

FROM RESEARCH TO SOUL SEARCH

Facts and interpretations gained from research are vital to the success of the elaborate lie you're concocting. But you should also use your story as a means of exploring your own inner mythology — of finding out why certain story elements or characters seem so important that you have to write about them.

I'm not suggesting that writing SF or fantasy is a form of therapy (though it may be), but that we should have some conscious understanding of our subconscious imagery. Authors, says Northrop Frye, are notoriously bad critics of their own work, but that doesn't mean we should just babble away and let others psychoanalyze us.

I'll try to explain what I mean by telling a couple of stories at my own expense. When I was a teenager cranking out space opera and Tolkien rip-offs, my brother was one of my first (and most withering) critics. "Your heroes are always too cool," he told me once.

It was true. They never got upset, they never choked in a crisis, and they never got nervous around girls. In other words, they were the way I wished I was — like the heroes in the pulp SF and fantasy stories I was devouring.

Sure, we want our characters to represent the best or worst of humanity, to be larger than life. But even Superman needs to be vulnerable to kryptonite, or he finally becomes too superhuman to be interesting.

A few years ago, a young writer named Samuel W. Fussell (son of the literary scholar and social critic Paul Fussell) wrote a fine book called *Muscle,* about his experience as a bodybuilder. Fussell turned himself into a giant for a very simple reason: he felt weak and vulnerable on the street. So he armored himself with muscle, making himself look too strong and dangerous to mess with. (He also made himself pretty sick from the diet required by serious bodybuilding.)

If you're yearning to write a fantasy about Thewbold the Barbarian, who makes Conan look like a wimp, ask yourself *why*. Why are sheer physical bulk and strength so interesting to you? Is Thewbold just some kind of human ballistic missile, unstoppable but unintelligent? Or is he, like Fussell, a scared young guy who's trying to protect himself in a dangerous world? If so, he's going to be a lot more interesting to many readers because we like to know the reasons for people's behavior, good or bad.

So my own characters, as I got older, became less cool — or their cool turned out to be a joke on them. My time-traveling hit man, Jerry Pierce, seems to be even worse than a cold-blooded killer: he actually feels virtuous when he "zaps a bad guy." What he doesn't know is that his own bosses are manipulating him, exploiting his subconscious need for love and acceptance, and the process is beginning to destroy him. Far from being cool, Jerry is a jerk.

In *Greenmagic,* my magician-hero Calindor is planning a kind of sorcerous coup against the Badakhar, the oppressors of his people. His weapon is the staff of another magician, which Calindor has managed to steal. Aware of its power (it contains entities called *sterkar,* which carry the force of magic), Calindor dreams of using it against the Badakhar; he even strokes it while promising the *sterkar* that soon he will release them.

Well, it took a female colleague, reading a draft of the story, to point out the phallic symbolism in Calindor's behavior. Was I ever embarrassed! But it was pretty funny because I'd been completely oblivious to that kind of reading, though I'd certainly seen such obvious symbolism in other writers' work.

An important part of soul search is to read and reread your manuscript as it develops. The manuscript is trying to tell you things —

not only about yourself and your subconscious, but about itself. Maybe your villain is becoming more likable than you expected or intended; perhaps you can understand his motives better, and even sympathize with them. That would not only reflect your own understanding but give you a chance to make your story more complex and subtle, more interesting to your readers.

Or you may find that your heroine, every time she's in a jam, has something witty to say. Maybe this means your subconscious finds something really funny about the situation you've put her in, and also means that your heroine has a better sense of humor than you'd planned on. Could it be that your story wants to be a satire instead of a dead-serious heroic fantasy or space opera?

Well, it could — but you're still the boss. If you don't want your heroine to be such a wit, because she's distracting from the dead-serious story you really want to tell, then step on all those one-liners of hers. Revise the scenes that turn unintentionally funny. In other words, use your subconscious to make yourself more conscious of what you're doing as a storyteller.

I ran into just such a problem in writing *Gryphon,* a space opera involving alien invasion. It turned into a tongue-in-cheek kind of war, with plenty of violence and destruction but not much solemnity. The result was a kind of deadpan satire on space opera that some readers, at least, just didn't get. If I'd done more soul search, the novel might have become much more funny, or much less. I guess I'll never know.

GETTING THE SCIENCE AND MAGIC RIGHT

The whole point of writing SF or fantasy is to look at our own world with some of the parameters changed — like looking at yourself in a fun house mirror, or wearing the clothes of the opposite sex, or having major plastic surgery.

But it's not just the brief shock of seeing ourselves differently; we can imagine ourselves looking different without actually going to the trouble of dressing up, or visiting the fun house, or going under the knife. Once we change the parameters, we should learn something we didn't expect, something startling and perhaps unsettling. We have not just imagined a world close to our heart's desire or demonically horrible — we now know our own hearts better, or we know our heart of darkness. Almost certainly, we'll learn that our fantasies of heaven and hell were far too simple. And once we've learned that, we return to our own world and look at it through different eyes.

To do that successfully, we first have to believe the story. We may be willing to play "let's pretend," but we don't want to pretend any more than absolutely necessary.

The Science in Science Fiction

In science fiction we pretend that humans have founded a colony on Mars, but it has to be the Mars that science shows us. The Barsoom of Edgar Rice Burroughs was Mars as understood (very poorly) by the astronomers who thought it had canals. That was good enough for Burroughs, who just needed an exotic setting for some old-fashioned thud-and-blunder adventures.

The Mars of Kim Stanley Robinson's trilogy is scientifically much more accurate, though future space missions will doubtless make Robinson's vision look as obsolete as Burroughs's. Robinson is also fond of adventure, but of a much more realistic kind. His characters are struggling to create and preserve a society, just as John Carter and Thuvia try to do in Burroughs's work, but it's a society we can recognize because it's so much like our own. If Robinson's science were bogus — for example, if his characters traveled along a canal — we'd reject the story no matter how good the other elements were.

What about "dated" classics like Robert Heinlein's *Red Planet, Double Star,* and *Stranger in a Strange Land,* which give us versions of Mars that we now know are impossible? Well, we can read them as we read fantasy (let's pretend Mars has water and life), or as we read *Gulliver's Travels* — more for the persistent themes of political conflict than for speculation on what living on Mars might really be like.

My point here is that the SF writer needs to know some basic science and live within its boundaries; but it's also critical to know what scientists themselves are speculating as they push into new territory. One good way to do this is to be a regular reader of periodicals such as *Science, Nature, Scientific American,* and *New Scientist.* Some of these magazines' articles will be incomprehensible, but others will make you feel ashamed of your own lack of imagination — while giving you some terrific ideas for your SF.

Scientists Isaac Asimov, Stephen Jay Gould, and Stephen Hawking have written brilliantly about what is on the edge of the known, or beyond. By all means read them, and pay special attention to what they reveal about the way science gets done. Gould was a superb historian of science, documenting the cultural biases of scientists; similar biases will surely influence the course of future science, which means your scientist characters will be as fallible, complicated, and human as Agassiz or Oppenheimer.

Intelligence (as the military defines it) is putting something that you know together with something else that you know, and coming up with something that you didn't previously know. That kind of intelligence is all too rare in SF, where writers make a couple of scientific assumptions (faster-than-light travel, alien contact) but leave everything else all too familiar. So, as I've noted earlier, we have interstellar fleets operating like World War II battleships, right down to the military bureaucracy running the fleets.

Hundreds of stories were written about the first lunar landing before it ever happened. They were scientifically plausible, for the time, and the characters were sometimes memorable. But as far as I know, not one such story imagined that the whole world would be watching on television when the first man stepped onto the lunar surface, or that the president would send his congratulations by radio. That was a failure of intelligence — not only scientific intelligence, but engineering and political intelligence as well.

I suggest, then, that you study a lot of science not just so you can sound plausible but so that you can also make connections that your readers haven't made, and will thank you for. (It's an old gag in SF that anyone can predict the automobile; the trick is to predict smog, traffic jams, and making out in the back seat.)

Once you have a fairly firm grasp of today's science, you can go ahead and develop some rules for your "future science." For example, if your characters use hyperspace to travel from star to star, work out how they do it. Do they need to get far away from a gravity well like the sun, or can they jump from their own living room to a comparable living room on Capella II? If that's the case, you don't need admirals commanding interstellar fleets — you just need a technician to press a button that lobs an H-bomb right into your enemy's house.

Too easy? Many SF writers seem to think so, so they create constraints on their future science. They make starflight through hyperspace depend on reaching deep space first, or they make it less than instant; maybe it takes 20 jumps to get from here to Capella, with time between jumps to figure out where to jump next. Or travel through hyperspace, while faster than light, still takes a lot of time — months or years.

Science That's Symbolically Right

Let me complicate your plans still more by suggesting your present science must not only be accurate; your future science must not only be constrained; but your science in general must be *symbolically appropriate*.

In other words, if just *getting* to Capella II is some kind of quest that challenges your characters, then your hyperspace science should require a long and difficult journey. If *being* on Capella II is the whole point of the story, because all the challenges take place there, then the journey can be instantaneous (or at any rate not part of your story).

More than that, the role of science in your world should reflect the society you are writing about. Has science become a kind of priesthood, concealing its secrets from the ignorant masses? Or has technology permitted everyone to do some kind of significant scientific research? Suppose you've chosen the priesthood option, and you approve of this approach; you can build your plot around your hero's efforts to join the priesthood and then to rise in it. (If you disapprove of science as priesthood, your hero can be expelled from his studies and then exercise science as a subversive outsider.)

The Magic in Fantasy

In one sense, magic is just dead science — a system of organizing knowledge on premises we now know to be wrong. But when our ancestors established those premises, they were usually concerned with explaining the world in terms that made humans — and human behavior — important.

This is especially true in the Western tradition, whether in the pagan Greek and Roman religions or the Judeo-Christian faiths that supplanted them. After all, God made us as we are, not just because we were an efficient design, or because our genome was on sale that week. He made us in His own image; we are morally significant members of a moral universe designed to make sense in terms we can understand.

Fantasy is equally concerned with evoking a morally meaningful universe; that's why many writers (and readers) prefer it to science fiction. In fantasy, meaning is not something we slap on from outside; it's built right into everything from the rocks and trees to the political system. The way to influence a morally meaningful universe is to understand and use magic.

Magic, therefore, has a strong moral component. If it's *white magic,* its effect is to help others improve in health, in spirit, or in general well-being (or at least to make the magician a better person). *Black magic* harms others, or gives the magician dangerous power over others — often at great risk to himself or herself. Technically, only a practitioner of black magic can be a sorcerer; in most modern fantasies, however, the term is interchangeable with terms such as magician, mage, warlock, and witch.

We can also distinguish between *high magic,* intended for the spiritual improvement of the magician, and *low magic,* which gets things done: it attracts a lover, drives away rats, makes crops grow better.

Low magic divides into further categories. It includes *natural magic,* which brings rain or sunshine, and *sexual magic,* which ensures fertility through ritualized sexual acts.

Magic uses ceremony and symbol to gain access to supernatural beings or powers. In high or white magic, the ritual carries the magician closer to divinity and some kind of mystical level of reality. In black magic, ritual brings demons or evil spirits into our world. The ritual may use an image, such as a wax figurine, as a means of *imitative magic:* to serve as the prison of an evil being that's possessed a human, for example, or to transmit harm from the image to the person it represents. Black magic may use images and spells as part of a *magical attack;* in that case, *protective magic* using counterspells is the only defense.

Whether high or low, black or white, magic is closely allied to language. The poet Kenneth Koch once demonstrated this in a class I took from him many years ago. He looked at one of us and said: "Would you stand up, please?" The student did so — and Koch, grinning delightedly, pointed out that simply by using a few words, he had performed an action at a distance, causing a big, strong young man to rise without the application of any physical force. Magic!

That explains why so many magic terms are also language terms: We cast a *spell*, for example. A *glamour* was originally a magic spell; it derives from *grammar,* which in turns derives from the Greek *grammatike,* literature. A *benediction* is a good saying or blessing; a *malediction,* or evil saying, is a curse. When we *conjure,* we literally "swear with." When we *invoke,* we "call in." If we add music, we have *enchantments and incantations; charm* comes from the Latin *carmen,* meaning song.

Unless you're setting your fantasy in a specifically European kind of world, you can of course use any kind of magic you like. But bear in mind that in some cultures, magic works like judo, getting the world to do what it wants to do anyway, only speeding things up. In others, magic is a way to break the world's rules, to make things happen against the law.

In *Greenmagic* and *Redmagic,* I used both kinds: the Cantareans' magic is organic, helping natural processes. The Badakhar practice a rougher magic that forces things to happen. Even rougher are the Exteca of *Redmagic,* whose use of human sacrifice gives them enormous magical power.

SETTING THE LIMITS OF MAGIC

As with science, your magic needs limits. Your characters can't solve every problem with a wave of their magic wands, or you have no story. As with the wish-fulfillment fantasy, achieving the power of magic should come at a high price.

In my fantasy novels the Badakhar magicians usually have addictive and obsessive personalities, always yearning to learn more magic and always jealous of other magicians. This is very convenient for everyone else, because otherwise the magicians would naturally seize political power. Instead they happily work for whichever warlord is ready to subsidize their quest for more magic. And they repay their masters by casting spells on other magicians, ensuring a general balance of power among the Badakhar kingdoms.

The Cantarean and Exteca magicians aren't quite as unpleasant as their Badakhar colleagues, but they too are fascinated by the intricacy of magic and mostly uninterested in anything else. This gives them limits and makes them much more useful as characters.

I suggested earlier that the theme of any SF or fantasy story is power and how to use it. Knowledge really is power, and science and magic are ways to organize knowledge. Even if your setting is exotically remote, and your science or magic is bizarre, your readers should recognize that your characters' use (and abuse) of knowledge has relevance to us in this world.

7

Elements of a Successful Story

If your novel or short story is going to work, it's going to need all the right components. Used without imagination or sensitivity, those elements may produce only formula fiction. But, like a good cook with the right materials and a good recipe, you can also create some pleasant surprises.

Many writers, like many good cooks, don't need to think consciously about what they're throwing in the pot. But as an apprentice you should probably think about how your story matches the following suggestions. They all have to do, essentially, with bringing your characters and readers from a state of ignorance to a state of awareness: Can your hero, an apprentice sorcerer, save her people from slavery without corrupting herself? We don't know, but we'll find out. Can your hero survive his reputation as a troublemaking, insubordinate young officer in the Starmarines and play a key role in defending the Terran Empire? We don't know, but we'll find out.

TOUGH QUESTIONS TO ASK YOURSELF

Before you start writing, ask yourself some tough questions:

(a) *How would I summarize my story on the dust jacket?* Would that summary interest casual readers enough to take my book to the cashier? Is the concept understandable? Does it make casual readers immediately wonder: How on earth would *that* turn out?

(b) *Is this story about the most critical time in my characters' lives?* If not, why aren't I writing about that time, instead of this one?

(c) *Is this story original in some important way?* Or is it just a stew of warmed-over clichés?

(d) *Is this story unpredictable?* It should be unpredictable right down to the minor details — your interplanetary assassin can't stand the sight of blood, he always gives in to his wife, his spacecraft smells bad.

(e) *Is this story realistic within the premises I've established, yet a little larger than life?* We want to read, after all, about a world that is closer to our daydreams, fantasies, or nightmares. Otherwise we'd be reading mainstream fiction.

Once you've got acceptable answers to those questions, you can start organizing the story itself.

THE OPENING

Remind yourself of the books you've picked off the shelf: Maybe the blurb on the back cover was intriguing, but within a page or two you were bored and the book went back on the shelf. Then think about the books that grabbed you on page one and wouldn't let you go. Chances are that the second kind of book followed certain rules.

Introduce Your Main Characters

Bring in your main characters, or at least foreshadow them. We might see your hero's mother getting married, for example, under conditions that doom her daughter to inherit a terrible talent for magic. Or we might see a starship destroyed under mysterious circumstances that will bring in your hero to investigate.

Foreshadow the Ending

Foreshadow the ending. If the hero is going to die in a storm of solar-flare radiation at the end, he may casually glance at the sun in the first chapter, or check his radiation badge. If it's a self-sacrificing death at the end, a similar death at the beginning may be accidental, or the result of criminal incompetence.

Show Characters under Stress

Show one or more characters under some kind of appropriate stress. For example, if your hero must perform well under telepathic assault in the climactic scene, show him being similarly assaulted in Chapter 1 — and performing badly. The story will then deal with his efforts to redeem himself and to prepare for a much more serious ordeal at the climax.

If the hero must resist temptation to use her sorcery for evil in the climactic confrontation, show her (or someone else) succumbing to such temptation in the beginning.

Whatever the cause of stress, bring it in at once. Your casual readers will go from the blurb on the dust jacket to the first page or two. If you can't hook them by page three, you're likely to lose them for good — just as many authors have lost you.

Show the Hero and the Villain

Show us who's the "good guy," who's the "bad guy." That is, in whom should we make an emotional investment? Whose side are we on? Even if your hero is morally repugnant (a criminal or a brutal warlord, for example), he should display some trait or attitude we can admire and identify with. The villain can be likable, maybe even well meaning, but set on a course we must reject. All your major characters should care intensely about something, and your good guys should care about other people.

Show What's at Stake

Editors and readers want to know this right away. (That's why the blurb on the jacket usually tells us: "Only one person can save humanity/defend the Galactic Empire/defeat the vampires ...") What does the hero stand to gain or lose personally? What's at stake for his or her family, community, society? What will happen if the villain wins?

When you foreshadow the ending in your opening pages, you can also show what's at stake. It should be a life-or-death issue for the main characters, and also for the societies they are defending, attacking, or trying to create. Suppose we see a sorcerer who succumbs to the temptation to use her power for evil, perhaps by telling herself it's evil in the service of good: she wants to protect her people from conquest or plague. But the spell backfires. Her rationalizing leads her to her own destruction, and to the destruction of the people she's trying to protect.

Your readers now know what can go wrong when a talented sorcerer misjudges herself and her powers. When they see your hero facing a similar temptation, they're going to feel anxious and uncomfortably involved in her decision.

Establish the Setting

Establish where and when the story takes place. If the setting is a space habitat or a domed city on Deimos, make this clear without a lot of clunky exposition. You'll show it to us through the eyes of one or more of your characters, who will usually take their surroundings for granted.

So if Mars is always visible through the dome over Deimopolis, your hero won't pay much attention to that huge rusty-red object in the sky; it's always been there. He may, however, gaze wistfully up at it when the lights of Sagan City are visible on Mars's nightside — because that's where his lost love has settled down with her new husband.

Establish the Scene of Conflict

If the setting is a space habitat that grows niche-market "wetware" (organic computer circuitry) at the turn of the 22nd century, the scene of conflict may be between designers and dealers, or within a family of designers, or within a single designer's personality.

The conflict should be understandable to us, but consistent with the different society you portray. A New York merchant in the 1780s wouldn't understand the details of a hostile New York takeover in the 1980s, least of all if it were a takeover of a company specializing in satellite communications or biotechnology. But the merchant would understand that money and power were at stake on a grand scale. In the same way, we will understand that control of some new wetware will bring enormous power — and with that power, a change in the nature of society itself, with more freedom or more oppression depending on who wins.

Set the Tone of the Story

Is your story going to be solemn or excited, humorous or tragic? The tone will depend much more on your characters' behavior than on your own narrative. If your characters' dialogue is full of wisecracks, or they swear by their children's blood to avenge their slain lord, your readers will respond accordingly. Bear in mind that your readers want a certain emotional experience. If they want to laugh, the wisecracks had better be funny. If they want to feel scared and awed, the ceremony of vengeance had better be deadly serious, performed by believably grim people.

But don't set a monotone! Ideally, your story should induce thrills, fear, grief, and laughter. Even Aragorn could crack a joke now and then, and your readers will be grateful for shifts in mood. When Hamlet goes into the graveyard, full of dour thoughts, the gravedigger gives him a few good one-liners and a much-needed new perspective.

THE BODY OF THE STORY

Your opening, whether a one-page prologue or a 10,000-word chapter, is the overture. You've established your themes, characters, and setting. Now the body of the story will show us what you only implied in the opening.

Use Scenes to Tell Your Story

The basic unit of the story is the scene. A scene contains a *purpose,* an *obstacle* or *conflict,* and a *resolution* that tells us something new about the characters and their circumstances. If your hero graduated from Starmarine Academy at the bottom of his class and nearly got kicked out for insubordination, don't tell us all that. Show us his first interview with his new commanding officer; she knows your hero's reputation and doesn't intend to let him get away with anything. Even at the level of the scene, something critical is at stake for these people; you have to show us what it is, and make us care.

What's more, both the hero and his new commanding officer should surprise us at least in some minor detail, revealing a degree of complexity we hadn't expected. Maybe they're instantly in conflict, but neither one can be stupid or insensitive or they never would have got this far.

Develop Your Characters through Action and Dialogue

Show us, don't tell us, what's going on and why. Don't write:

> He was an insubordinate shavetail.

when you can write:

> "I'll obey every legitimate order I'm given," he replied, and paused for half a second. "Ma'am."

Include All the Elements Needed for the Conclusion

On the ancient Greek stage, when the characters got themselves into a total mess, a god would descend (in a box on a rope) from Olympus to sort things out. This was the original *deus ex machina,* the "god out of the machine" that resolved the story. This kind of unprepared-for ending is no longer acceptable. It includes props and character traits that we haven't been shown before the climax.

If everything depends on killing the villain with a crossbow, show us the crossbow long before your hero has to pick it up and use it. But don't telegraph your punch. The crossbow should be just one of many items your readers encounter; they shouldn't see it as crucial to the outcome.

This applies to character traits as well: A total coward can't suddenly become brave enough to pick up the crossbow unless stress has forced him to exercise courage that's been at least faintly hinted at earlier in the story.

Give Your Characters Real Motivation

Drama is people doing amazing things for very good reasons. Melodrama is people doing amazing things for bad, stupid, trivial, or nonexistent reasons. Stick with drama.

For one thing, it makes your characters more interesting, because people usually do amazing things only because some painful inner insecurity goads them into action. What scares them also motivates them.

So if your sorcerer feels tempted to use an evil spell, it may be because she isn't entirely confident of the power of good spells or of her own magical talents. Perhaps she was enslaved as a child. And she identifies so strongly with her people that the thought of their being enslaved makes her desperate enough to try anything.

Remember that the basic theme of science fiction and fantasy is power and how to use it. The greater the power your characters can exert, the less sure of themselves they should be. (You can define a villain as someone who uses power with too much confidence and too little caution — someone who really is behaving melodramatically, acting out of foolish or trivial reasons.)

Develop the Plot as a Series of Increasingly Serious Problems

Your characters are going from the frying pan to the fire and then to the blast furnace. Each solution tells us more about the characters and their situation, but it also raises the stakes. The hero escaped the warlord's assassins in Chapter 5 by fleeing into the snowy mountains; now, in Chapter 6, she risks death in an avalanche.

Create Suspense

Make the solutions of your characters' problems uncertain. How will the hero escape the avalanche and then avoid freezing to death in Chapter 7?

Those solutions should be appropriate to the characters, and should reveal new aspects of their personalities. When we saw the hero graduate from mountain-commando training in Chapter 1, we didn't expect she'd put her skills to use quite so soon.

Show Your Characters Changing

After everything you've put them through, your characters would be brain-dead if they didn't change. Maybe they're still heading for their original goal, but for very different reasons, and with a very different understanding of themselves. We should share and appreciate that understanding, which means their experience is also changing us. (You might almost define formula fiction as a story that fails to change its readers.)

Take Your Characters into the Depths of Despair

At some point, all is lost. The spell has failed, the plague has escaped the laboratory, the interplanetary assassin has killed the prime minister, and the coup has begun. The triumph of evil seems assured. Do it right, and your readers will feel as if turning the page is suicidal ... but they'll turn it anyway.

That's because they're looking for the *counterthrust*. On the level of the individual scene, the counterthrust is the character's response to a challenge. On the level of the whole story, the counterthrust is the hero's Plan B. The original plan has gone nowhere, but the hero has learned something from that failure. She can't rely on the ancient amulet, or the division of Starmarines she'd been counting on, but some resource, until now unrecognized, is still available to her.

THE CONCLUSION

Present a Final, Crucial Conflict

Everything gained so far, at such cost, is in danger. It could be lost by a single word or deed: this is the climax, which reveals something to your readers (and perhaps to your characters) that has been implicit from the outset but not obvious or predictable. If you began with a single dramatic scene revealing one aspect of your characters and their predicament, the climax should come as the final knock-out blow after a rapid sequence of revelations, each of which makes us look at the characters in a new light but also leaves us too staggered to reflect much before the next shock hits. After all, just moments ago we were in the depths of despair.

The climax is the final proof of your myth: that a woman in love will stick with her lover at any cost, that simple decency can overthrow tyrants, that we can escape the dead hand of the past if we're brave and determined enough.

THROUGHOUT THE STORY

Just as a concerto has movements, and a play has acts, your story has a beginning, middle, and end. But some elements should appear consistently throughout the story.

Everything Has a Reason

Remember that nothing in a story happens at random. Why is the hero's name Sophia? Why is she a witch? Why is her familiar a black Lab instead of a black cat?

The easy answer is that you're the god of your novel and that's the way you want things. Better said, it's the way your subconscious wants things. But if you have a conscious reason for these elements, the story gains in interest because it carries more meaning. For example, "Sophia" means "wisdom" and the name can provide a cue to readers — maybe an ironic one, if your Sophia is not a very wise witch, or wisdom is beside the point in her particular predicament.

Use Images, Metaphors, and Similes Deliberately

Never use a phrase just because it "sounds good." Your style is actually a storytelling device, showing us something about your characters and their world. (Think about the banal language of the characters in Stanley Kubrick's *2001: A Space Odyssey,* or the corrupted English of San Lorenzo in Vonnegut's *Cat's Cradle.*) Choosing the right style is especially important in fantasy, where high diction can bloat into palpitating purple prose in the blink of a gargoyle's eye. Maintain consistent style, tone, and point of view (see Chapter 11 for more details on point of view).

The American author Cormac McCarthy, in his 2006 novel *The Road,* seriously violates this rule, and not to good effect. His highly educated nameless protagonist thinks in a rich vocabulary. But he speaks with his son in a flat style bordering on clichés. (For a detailed discussion of this novel, see my review in *The Tyee:* http://thetyee.ca/Books/2006/12/06/TheRoad/. This link and many other links to websites are provided on the CD that came with this book.)

Style results from using a particular vocabulary and sentence rhythms to tell a particular kind of story. Imagine telling a military-SF novel in the style of *The Lord of the Rings* (or vice versa), and you can see what an impact style can have on a story.

Tone is a specific aspect of style that expresses the "emotional climate" of your story — solemn, suspenseful, humorous, ironic, horrifying. While tone may change with your characters' emotions, try to keep an underlying consistency.

Point of view is usually consistent at least within a given scene. If you're showing us how your young sorcerer is reacting to the sight of her first demon, don't switch in midscene to the demon's point of view.

Know the Conventions of Your Chosen Form

Every genre has its own conventions, and you should break them — but only when you have a good reason to. For example, if it's conventional for the warlord of a nomad horde to be an aggressive, hard-drinking polygamist, you're going to surprise readers if your warlord is a shy, yogurt-loving teenager and a bit of a mama's boy.

You'll surprise readers even more if he goes around beheading people. As a warlord, his behavior will still depend on his personality and limitations: if he beheads people, it's only to make Mama happy.

Of course you can include all these elements and still end up with a dull, predictable, formula-driven story. The vital ingredient is always the author's own imagination. And no doubt you could cite plenty of successful stories and novels that don't contain all these elements. Chances are their authors were either deeply experienced writers or simply much more talented than you and I could ever hope to be.

Perhaps you're eager to break convention, tinker with the formula, and establish yourself as a courageous innovator in your genre. If so, congratulations and good luck. But first know how these story elements function, and abandon them only when you have a very good, very clear reason as a storyteller for doing so. If you flout convention only to show off, your readers will have a very good, very clear reason to abandon you.

8

Developing Characters

Science fiction and fantasy are widely condemned for their "cardboard" characters. To a certain extent, it's a deserved verdict. These genres descend from earlier genres in which the idea or setting is the main focus, like the utopias of classical Menippean satire. But a good story is always better if we can understand and value its characters.

WHAT MAKES A BELIEVABLE CHARACTER?

Plausible, complex characters are crucial to successful storytelling. You can develop them in several ways.

Concreteness

Giving characters concreteness means that they have specific homes, possessions, medical histories, tastes in furniture, political opinions. Apart from creating verisimilitude (the appearance of truth), these concrete aspects of the characters should convey information about the story: Does the hero smoke Marlboros because he's a rugged outdoorsman, or because that's the brand smoked by men of his social background, or just because you happen to smoke them?

Symbolic Association

You can express a character's nature metaphorically through objects or settings (a rusty sword, an apple orchard in bloom, a violent thunderstorm). At first these may not be perfectly understandable to the reader (or to the writer!), but they seem subconsciously right. Symbolic associations can be consciously "archetypal," linking the character to similar characters in literature.

Or you may use symbols in some private system that the reader may or may not consciously grasp. Characters' names can form symbolic associations, though this practice has become less popular in modern fiction except in comic or ironic writing.

Speech

The character's speech (both content and manner) helps to evoke personality: shy and reticent, aggressive and frank, coy and humorous. Both content and manner of speech should accurately reflect the character's social and ethnic background, without stereotyping. This is a matter of vocabulary and speech rhythms, not of phonetic spelling. If a character "speaks prose," his or her background should justify that rather artificial manner. If a character is inarticulate, that itself should convey something.

Behavior

From table manners to performance in hand-to-hand combat, each new example of behavior should be consistent with what we already know of the character, yet it should reveal some new aspect of his or her personality. Behavior under different forms of stress should be especially revealing. The fearless warrior on the battlefield may be terrified of expressing his love to the queen (especially if she's still married to the king).

Motivation

The characters should have good and sufficient reasons for their actions, and should carry those actions out with plausible skills. If we don't believe characters would do what the author tells us they do, the story fails.

Bear in mind that the characters' motivation may not be something your readers will automatically sympathize with. An ironic character has less freedom and knowledge than we do. Such a character's motivation may amuse us or disgust us — but we should still be able to understand that motivation.

Change

Characters should respond to their experiences by changing — or by working hard to avoid changing. As they try to carry out their agendas, run into conflicts, fail or succeed, and confront new problems, they will not stay the same people. If a character seems the same at the end of a story as at the beginning, readers at least should be changed and be aware of whatever factors kept the character from growing and developing.

THE CHARACTER RÉSUMÉ

One useful way to learn more about your characters is to fill out a "résumé" for them like that shown in Worksheet 1. You may not use all this information, and you may want to add categories of your own, but a résumé certainly helps make your character come alive in your own mind. Again, remember to ask yourself *why* the character is of a particular ethnic background, or of a particular age or education. The particulars could trigger (and perhaps challenge) readers' stereotypes; that's a response that you as writer must reckon with.

The résumé can also give you helpful ideas on everything from explaining the character's motivation to conceiving incidents that dramatize the character's personal traits. You may find that your characters tell you about themselves as you write, and you can include what you learn in their résumés. It's often easier to consult your project bible about such traits rather than riffle through the manuscript to remind yourself of the countless details you need to keep straight.

WORKSHEET I
CHARACTER RÉSUMÉ

Name:_____

_____

Address & phone number:_____

_____

_____

Date & place of birth:_____

_____

_____

Height/weight/physical description:_____

_____

_____

Citizenship/ethnic origin:_____

_____

Parents' names & occupations:_____

_____

_____

_____

Other family members:_____

_____

_____

_____

_____

_____

Spouse or lover & occupation:_____

_____

_____

Friends' names & occupations:_____

_____

_____

_____

Social class:_____

_____

Education:_____

_____

Occupation/employer:_____

_____

_____

Social class:_____

_____

Salary:_____

_____

Community status:_____

_____

Job-related skills:_____

_____

_____

Political beliefs/affiliations:_____

_____

Hobbies/recreations:_____

_____

Personal qualities (imagination, taste, etc.):_____

_____

_____

Ambitions:_____

_____

Fears/anxieties/hangups:_____

_____

Intelligence:_____

_____

Sense of humor:_____

_____

Most painful setback/disappointment:_____

_____

Most instructive/meaningful experience:_____

_____

_____

Health/physical condition/distinguishing marks/disabilities:___

_____

_____

Sexual orientation/experience/values:_____

_____

_____

Tastes in food, drink, art, music, literature, décor, clothing:___

_____

_____

Attitude toward life:_____

_____

Attitude toward death:_____

_____

Philosophy of life (in a phrase):_____

_____

9
Plotting

Plotting drives many writers crazy. They can't seem to find enough for their characters to do, or reasons for them to do it. They feel their characters are wandering around aimlessly, without so much as a theme, let alone a goal.

That was the problem a student brought to me a few years ago. She was writing a romance about a torrid affair between a legal secretary and a rock star. She herself was a legal secretary, so this was an entertaining form of daydreaming in print, but the daydream wasn't getting anywhere.

That was because she wasn't giving her characters enough problems. So I suggested ways to make her lovers' lives absolutely miserable.

Give the secretary a boss whose legal practice is on its last legs, I told her. She may be out of a job at any moment because her boss can't find enough work. And put her in a town where legal secretaries are fighting each other for jobs.

Then, when she and her new sweetie come up for air and start to get acquainted, she learns he's locked into a lousy contract that pays him almost nothing and forces him to go on the road all the time — and our hero wants to keep him close at hand. What's more, in the story most of the local rock musicians are tied into similar contracts framed by unscrupulous managers and record-company executives.

When her boss and her boyfriend both face the ruin of their careers, our hero introduces them. Boss shows boyfriend how to fight and break his contract. Boyfriend not only gets a better contract; other musicians swarm in, demanding similar help. Boss launches a hot new career in entertainment law, while boyfriend makes pots of money and our hero becomes his new manager.

See how easy it is when you give your characters lots of trouble? And we could complicate the plot still more if lawyer and rocker start to compete for our hero …

Just make sure that none of your characters put up with their misery for very long, because plots consist of people fighting back against adversity. With this example in mind, let's look at ten basic principles of plotting.

BASIC PRINCIPLES OF PLOTTING

Nothing Should Happen at Random

Ideally, a short story or novel should have the symbolic intensity and complexity of a poem; in reality, we all fall short (and so do most poets). Every element in a story should have significance, whether for verisimilitude, symbolism, or the intended climax. Names, places, actions, and events should all be purposeful. To test the significance of an element, ask yourself: Why are the aliens from Alpha

Centauri and not from Barnard's Star? Why are they semireptilian and not insectoid? Why do they want to invade when Earth is so different from their own world? Why is the hero seemingly sympathetic to them? Whatever the questions, the answers should be:

(a) to persuade readers of the story's plausibility,

(b) to convey a message about the theme of the story, and

(c) to prepare readers for the climax so that it seems both plausible and in keeping with the theme.

Plot Stems from Character under Adversity

When we're under enough stress, we reveal our true selves, good or bad. Since your story is at bottom a quest for identity, you are by definition looking for your characters' true selves, so you have to stress them without mercy. But you have to do it carefully and believably. A mild-mannered person can't achieve his or her goals with an out-of-character action like a violent assault, unless we have prepared readers for it by revealing a glimpse of some suppressed aspect of that character's personality that can be plausibly released by stress.

And the stress itself must also be plausible, given the circumstances of the story. Once we believe that your hero Michael Milquetoast is wrestling with demons, *then* you can show Michael suddenly losing his battle and going berserk. If we haven't seen the demons, *we'll* go berserk and throw your book across the room.

Each Character Has an Urgent Personal Agenda

Too much is at stake for a character to abandon his or her agenda without good reason. We may not share the character's urgency, but we should be able to see why he or she cares so much about what he or she is doing. A character who acts without real motivation is by definition melodramatic, doing outrageous things for the sake of the thrill it gives readers — not because it makes sense for the character to do so.

Remember that your characters are exiled from paradise and fighting to regain paradise by changing (or escaping from) the demonic world they now find themselves in. They have lost something immeasurably precious, and their lives are now terrifyingly insecure. Compromise is out of the question, so the stakes are high.

The Story's Plot Is the Synthesis of Its Individual Characters' Plots

Each character has a personal agenda, modified by conflict or harmony with the agendas of others. The villain doesn't get everything his or her way, any more than the hero does; each keeps thwarting the other, who must then improvise under pressure. Your villain wants to go south, and your hero wants to go east; after their first collision, they will be locked together and traveling southeast, where neither wants to go.

The Plot Begins Long before the Story

Especially if the stakes are high and some immense effort is involved, the antagonists have been preparing for months, years, maybe centuries. But you'll sabotage your story if you plod through every step of the preparations.

The story itself should begin at *the latest possible moment before the climax,* at some point when events take a decisive and irreversible turn. If your hero misses the Singapore-Vancouver hyperjet shuttle, the story won't happen; if she's on board, the story is as inevitable as the hyperjet's trajectory. We may learn later, through flashbacks, exposition, or inference, about events occurring before the beginning of the story — but only as much as we need to. Tolkien spends much of his great trilogy reviewing the long and complex history that has culminated in Frodo's leaving the Shire with the Ring. But unless you're telling an equally vast epic, you shouldn't need that much explanation.

Foreshadow All Important Elements

The first part of a story, Northrop Frye tells us, is a kind of prophecy; the second part fulfills the prophecy. Any important character, location, or object should be foreshadowed early in the story. (This is why the Russian playwright Anton Chekhov used to say that if the curtain goes up in Act I showing a living room with a shotgun hanging above the mantel, by the time the curtain comes down at the end of the play, someone had better fire that shotgun.)

You can foreshadow, but you shouldn't telegraph your punch either. Your readers don't want to see what's coming, especially if your characters seem too dumb to see it themselves. The trick is to put the plot element into your story without making readers excessively aware of its importance. But when the foreshadowing pays off and the prophecy is fulfilled, readers should say to themselves, "Wow — of course! Why didn't I see it coming?"

Chance and coincidence, in particular, require careful preparation if they are going to influence the plot. In other words, show us minor events that happen by coincidence, and show us your characters reflecting on those coincidences, so we're prepared for the major coincidence your story hinges on.

Keep in Mind the Kind of Story You're Telling

Any story is about the relationship of an individual to society, a relationship that defines the individual's identity. A *comic* story describes an isolated individual achieving social integration either by being accepted into an existing society or by forming his or her own. This integration is sometimes symbolized by a wedding or feast. A *tragic story* describes an integrated individual who becomes isolated; death is simply a symbol of this isolation.

The plot should keep us in some degree of suspense about what kind of story we're reading. Even if we know it's a comedy, the precise nature of the comic climax should come as a surprise. If we know the hero is doomed, his or her downfall should stem from a factor we know about but have not given sufficient weight to.

Ironic Plots Subvert Their Surface Meanings

When ironic plots subvert their surface meanings, an ordinarily desirable goal appears very unattractive to us: in George Orwell's *Nineteen Eighty-Four,* Winston Smith, finally reconciled to the politics of Oceania, loves Big Brother. But his integration into a demonic society turns his story into a tragedy. Or an undesirable outcome, like the hero's death, is actually the best thing that could happen for the hero and his or her society.

Science fiction and fantasy, with their roots in satire, can thrive on irony; its crudest form is parody, like Terry Pratchett's send-ups of formula fantasy. Its most sophisticated form is perhaps that of Orwell. He never openly reveals that Winston Smith is a mere plaything of O'Brien, who has completely scripted Winston's pathetic revolt and his love for Julia, just for the pleasure of destroying him.

The Hero Must Eventually Take Charge of Events

In any plot, the hero is passive for a time, reacting to highly stressful events. At some point he or she must try to take charge. This is the *counterthrust,* when the story goes into high gear. In some cases, we may have a series of thrusts and counterthrusts; in the opening stages of the plot, the counterthrust helps define the hero's character and puts him or her in position for more serious conflicts (and counterthrusts) later in the story.

You could even say that *every scene* presents the hero with a problem; the hero's response, successful or not, is his or her counterthrust. In the larger structure of the plot, the counterthrust often comes after the hero's original plan of action has failed; he or she has learned some hard lessons and now will apply them as he or she approaches the climax of the story.

Plot Dramatizes Character

If all literature is the story of the quest for identity, then plot is the road map of that quest. Every event, every response, should reveal (to us if not to them) some aspect of the characters' identities. Plot elements dramatize characters' identities by providing opportunities to be brave or cowardly, stupid or brilliant, generous or mean.

These opportunities come in the form of severe stress, appropriate to the kind of story you're telling. A plot element used for its own sake — a fistfight, a sexual encounter, an ominous prophecy — is a needless burden to the story if it does not illuminate the characters involved. Conversely, readers will not believe any character trait that you have not dramatized through a plot device.

WHAT TO DO WITH YOUR PLOT ELEMENTS

Storyboarding: Organizing Your Plot

"Storyboarding" usually means arranging a sequence of images for a film or commercial. But you can storyboard a novel or short story also, and it can be a helpful way to organize the plot.

That's because we don't normally think in terms of plot. Suppose you have an idea for a story, "Wolfmaster" (genetically engineered boy can communicate telepathically, but only with wolves, coyotes, and dogs), and a random assortment of mental images that grip you emotionally (encounter with a dying wolf leader, wild ride to rescue pack from hunters, gorgeous blonde swimming nude in icy stream, showdown with genetic engineers who want to retrofit him with antitelepathy gene). How do you get from that to a coherent plot?

Writing a letter to yourself may help, but first try this: Take a stack of three-by-five-inch cards and jot down an image or scene on each one, just in the order the ideas occur to you. It might look something like this:

> *Jesse summons wolves to*
> *rescue him by attacking*
> *soldiers escorting him from*
> *jail to Humvee.*

When you have 5 or 10 or 20 such cards, lay them out in the sequence you envisage for the story. You certainly don't have a card for each scene in the novel, but you have the scenes that your subconscious seems to want to deal with.

You also have numerous gaps. How do you get Jesse from his laboratory-home in Nevada to the wolf pack in northern Idaho? How does Caleb Sanders, the laboratory chief, get in touch with the three hired killers from San Francisco? How does Jesse respond to the death of the pack leader?

Now you turn your thoughts to just those gaps, and new ideas occur to you. That means more cards. Maybe some of the new ideas are better than the original ones, so some of the old cards go in the trash. New characters emerge to fulfill functions in the story. Your research into genetic engineering and canine behavior suggests still more scenes which might go into this or that part of the novel; still more cards go into your growing deck.

The story may eventually end up as a series of flashbacks, but for now stick to straight chronological order. Maybe the whole story occurs during a three-hour siege in a remote Idaho canyon where Jesse and the wolves have holed up; maybe it stretches across three decades and a continent.

Whatever the "real time" of your story, you may see that the cards clump naturally around certain periods of the plot and you see no need for events to fill in the gaps. That's fine; maybe you've found the natural divisions between chapters or sections of the story.

Keep asking yourself *why*. Why Nevada, why telepathy with dogs, why a gorgeous naked blonde in a freezing river? Don't keep a scene in your storyboard unless you can justify it as a way to —

(a) dramatize a character's personality,

(b) move the story ahead, and

(c) lend verisimilitude.

If you absolutely must have a scene in which Jesse's true love Amanda goes wading naked in an icy creek and then nearly drowns, what good will the scene do for the story? Does it show us that Amanda wants to prove how tough she is? Does it move the story ahead by revealing something that will pay off later in the story, like the fact that Amanda is a very bad swimmer? Does it make the story more believable — by showing how crossing a stream naked, with your clothes above your head, means you at least have dry clothes to get back into on the other side?

Once you have at least the main sequence of events clearly mapped out on your cards, you can begin to transfer them to a more manageable outline. Your outline may be highly detailed or very sketchy. It can be on three-by-five-inch cards, or on the back of an envelope, or in a separate file in your computer — whatever you find most convenient for regular review and modification.

 CREATING SCENES

As you begin each new chapter, start by listing the events or scenes from your outline that you intend to include in the chapter. Erase these reminders as you complete the scenes. Chances are that you'll find you've listed more than the completed chapter can really hold, so now you know what scenes to use at the start of the next chapter!

Thickening Your Plot

Building a plot is easier than you may think. It consists of putting believable characters in believable situations and then making their lives unbelievably difficult. So at each stage of your story, throw in a complication:

1. Create a plausible setting in which we could expect to find a person like your hero; for example, a desert where water divining is the highest magic and where the hero is a boy who shows promise in the art.

2. Complication: Bring in a drought that makes the desert uninhabitable. But also bring in powerful mountain-dwelling neighbors who kidnap all the water diviners, including the hero's sister.

3. Complication: Hero must choose to rescue sister, or stay and help people find more water. (Tip: At this point, the decision is always going to be the wrong one.) Hero chooses to rescue sister.

4. Complication: Painful journey into enemy territory, with a series of reverses that leave the hero unable to rescue sister or to go home. In each adventure, however, the hero's divining powers increase. He finds he can call water out of dry springs, riverbeds, and so on.

5. Complication: Hero can go home with new powers, bring water to the desert, and rescue the people. He rejects this because he's loyal to his sister.

6. Complication: But now what? The hero's people are dying, his sister is in captivity, and the mountain people will eventually run out of water regardless.

7. Complication: Hero allows himself to be captured, taken to fortress where the other diviners are imprisoned. His plan: Teach other diviners how to call forth water, then use it to bargain for freedom.

8. Complication: Sister's fallen in love with mountaineer prince, doesn't want to be liberated.

9. Complication: Hero learns prince is trifling with sister, doesn't really love her, but sister refuses to believe the truth.

10. Complication: Hero teaches other diviners how to call forth water; together, they create a cloudburst and enormous floods, and plan to escape in the storm.

11. Complication: Hero can't leave sister behind, though storm threatens to destroy fortress.

12. Complication: Prince and hero confront each other in the flooded fortress, which is collapsing. Prince is about to kill hero, and reveals that he doesn't love hero's sister. She overhears, and furiously calls forth a still greater downpour that sweeps the prince to his death. Hero and sister, reconciled, escape from ruined fortress. They promise surviving mountaineers that the drought is over and everyone will have enough water from now on.

Time needed to create this plot: Less than half an hour. Just keep your characters in trouble, and make them imaginative enough to get out of it, and plotting will take care of itself.

10

Constructing a Scene

The basic unit of fiction is not the sentence or the paragraph, but the scene.

Every scene in a story has both a verbal and a nonverbal content. The verbal content may be a young man courting a girl, or the president of the United States deciding whether to go ahead with a nuclear attack on a biological-warfare research center. The nonverbal content is concealed in the way you present the scene: you want your readers to think that the young man is touchingly awkward, or obnoxiously crude; that the president is a shallow twerp or a deeply sensitive man facing a terrible decision.

In effect, you are like an attorney presenting a case to the jury. You supply the evidence, and the jury supplies the verdict. If you *tell* us that the young man is touchingly awkward, we may well disbelieve you. But if you *show* us his awkward behavior, and we say, "Aw, the poor lunk!" — then your scene has succeeded.

Every scene presents a problem of some kind for one or more characters, and shows us how the characters deal with that problem. That, in turn, shows us something about the characters and moves the story ahead.

Here's an exercise you may find useful. Take about 30 minutes to write a scene that dramatizes the elements given here, and that leads to a decisive resolution:

- A riot in the town marketplace, instigated by foreign agents hostile to your hero, Prince Manoduro;

- Chando Bartak, a 23-year-old mercenary: male chauvinist, aggressive personality, with no love for the prince or for the foreigners;

- Manzana, a 22-year-old farm girl with a stall in the market: worried about making money for her family, able to make friends easily, knows the city well, has a slight gift for "songspells" — enchantments that last only for the length of the song;

- The need to get Chando from the marketplace to the prince's palace with vital information about the identity of the rioters, when he's seriously outnumbered and prone to impulsive violence.

Give yourself just half an hour to write such a scene, so that readers will finish reading it knowing all this information. I predict you'll be amazed at how quickly you can produce such a scene, and at how it leads logically to another scene. (You may also be appalled at your own speed, if writing such a scene normally takes you hours or days.)

You just have to know what you want to show your readers about your characters and their problems. Once you know that, everything else follows pretty easily.

So consider what's going on in your own story. What do you want your readers to think about your hero? That she's shy but determined? That she thinks no man could ever love her? That she's perceptive about other women but baffled by men? Whatever those traits may be, you should be able to think of logical, plausible events that could force her to show them to us.

INTRODUCING CHARACTERS

If your plot demands a fairly large cast — for example, your hero is the commanding officer of a Starmarine platoon or the matriarch of a noble family — don't introduce a whole mob of characters at once. Bring in your protagonist first, in a scene that demonstrates the character's key traits (e.g., courage, leadership, self-hatred). Then bring in each of the supporting characters in a scene that lets them display their key traits as well, while deepening our understanding of the protagonist.

This way you build up interest in the story by building up interest in your varied and complex characters, as Tolkien does in *The Lord of the Rings*.

In some cases, your plot will give you some automatic scenes. If your hero is traveling by shuttle from Sagan City on Mars up to an orbiting interplanetary liner, maybe her seatmate is an attractive man who studiously ignores her; maybe the liner's captain gives her a hard time but she insists on her rights; maybe your hero sees the attractive man greeted by a woman he seems to dote on even though your perceptive hero can see the woman despises him. And so on.

How long should a scene be? Long enough to make its point. A scene may run to just a sentence or two, or it may take up 20 pages. When it ends, we should know more about the characters involved, and their problems should have increased. This doesn't mean endlessly increasing gloom, but it means that even a character achieving his or her goal only clears the way for a more stressful scene to come. Your young mercenary Chando may kill the rioters' ringleader in the marketplace, but the death will make Chando a marked man; now the rioters will try to kill him.

How many characters should take part in a scene? As few as possible. Even a debate in the U.S. Congress isn't going to involve every last representative.

And how do we jump to the next scene? That depends on the kind of story you're telling. If you've got two or more plot strands going at once, separated by great distances, you can maintain some suspense by ending one scene with something uncertain (the old cliffhanger gimmick) while switching from that scene's locale to another. When the second scene is over, you switch back to locale number one.

But remember that each scene resolves a problem while setting the characters up for a still more serious problem. If you're telling your story in third person omniscient (discussed in detail in the next chapter), you might have a scene between Chando and Manzana, from Chando's point of view. He's solved a problem, and ended the scene by killing a rioter as he and Manzana are trying to escape the marketplace, and now the rioters are hard on their heels.

The next scene follows immediately after, but now the point of view is Manzana's as she hauls Chando into a maze of alleys in an attempt to escape without further bloodshed. Even if they get to Prince Manoduro's palace, Chando's impulsive act is going to put him in deep trouble — which he or Manzana will have to find a way out of.

11

Narrative Voice

Someone in your story has to tell us that Jeff pulled out his gun, that Samantha smiled at the tall stranger, that daylight was breaking over Copernicus Dome. That someone is the narrator, or author's persona.

The author's persona of a fictional narrative can help or hinder the success of the story. Which persona you adopt depends on what kind of story you are trying to tell and what kind of emotional atmosphere works best for the story.

The persona develops from the personality and attitude of the narrator, which are expressed by the narrator's choice of words and incidents. These in turn depend on the point of view of the story. If the narrator is in the story, and happens to be a female officer in the Starmarines, we expect her to sound both "military" and "feminine" (as the author wants to define those traits in the story).

If the narrator is just the author telling a story in the third person, the persona is less clearly defined; it may be a lot like the author himself or herself, or very different. But the persona will still tell readers what's happening in the story and what kind of attitude they should adopt toward events. For example, the persona may describe a death and make us feel outraged, or horrified, or amused.

FIRST PERSON POINT OF VIEW

First person point of view is usually subjective: readers learn the narrator's thoughts, feelings, and reactions to events. The narrator may be a keen observer of other people's behavior, so readers get good insights into their emotions as well. Or the narrator may be maddeningly obtuse, and doesn't even understand what he or she's reporting, as with the unreliable narrator.

Unreliable Narrator

In some cases, the narrator is not only obtuse but is plain lying or at least distorting events, and readers have to spot the inconsistencies in the story.

This technique, which tells us more than the narrator knows (or wants us to know) is called the unreliable narrator; it's a good way to dramatize a dishonest or limited personality.

First Person Objective

In first person objective, however, the narrator tells us only what people said and did, without comment, and leaves it up to readers to imagine what they were feeling:

> I aimed the laser at his chest. The red dot showed up clearly on the scope. I squeezed the trigger and he fell. His shirt was on fire but he didn't move.

This may help to dramatize a sociopathic, unemotional character, but it can also seem coldly manipulative, and even a challenge to readers: Can you be as tough as I am about inflicting and witnessing death?

Observer Narrator

An observer narrator is a narrator outside the main story (such as Fido, the first person narrator in *Odd John* by Olaf Stapledon). This type of narrator is useful when the intense emotions of the main characters are too "hot" and hard to accept if we're up close to them.

Detached Autobiography

A detached autobiography narrator is a narrator looking back on long-past events, with the benefit of hindsight. This type of narrator is especially effective if the narrator is confessing something, like Montresor in Edgar Allan Poe's "The Cask of Amontillado."

Multiple Narrators

Multiple narrators are first person accounts by several characters. In the Japanese film *Rashomon,* each narrator has a different version of a murder, even the ghost of the murdered man. This kind of narration works well if you're trying to show how "reality" depends on one's point of view.

Interior Monologue

An interior monologue is one in which the narrator recounts the story as a memory (stream of consciousness is an extreme form of this narrative). This kind of narration carries us along with the character's own journey of self-discovery, and readers may end up knowing more than the character does.

Dramatic Monologue

In a dramatic monologue, the narrator tells the story out loud without interruption. This is the form used in Sir Arthur C. Clarke's *Tales from the White Hart,* unlikely stories related in an equally unlikely pub.

Letter/Diary Narrative

With letter/diary narrative, the narrator writes down events as they happen. One of the first forms of narrative in the 18th-century novel, this "epistolary" form is enjoying a mild comeback in stories told through exchanges of email.

If the point of view is first person, questions about the persona are simple: the character narrating the story has a particular personality and attitude, plausibly expressed by the way he or she describes events. The trick for the novice author is what actors call "staying in character." It's fatally easy to slip into your own character, so the narrator sounds just like you.

Another hazard is making the first person narrator so different from yourself (and from your readers) that it's hard to figure out what's going on. This is the case in Iain Banks's *Feersum Endjinn,* part of which is narrated by an alien with a tedious fondness for phonetic spelling.

SECOND PERSON POINT OF VIEW

The second person mode is rare: *You knocked on the door. You went inside.* Very few writers feel the need for it, and still fewer use it effectively.

THIRD PERSON POINT OF VIEW

Chances are that you'll find third person the most effective point of view for telling your story. And within third person you have several useful choices.

Third Person Limited

If the point of view is third person limited, persona again depends on the single character through whose eyes readers witness the story. You may go inside the character's mind and tell us how that character thinks and feels, or you may describe outside events in terms the character would use. Readers like this point of view because they know whom to invest in or identify with.

Third Person Objective

In third person objective, readers have no entry to anyone's thoughts or feelings. The author simply describes, without emotion or editorializing, what the characters say and do. The author's persona here is almost nonexistent. Readers may be unsure whose fate they should care about, but it can be very powerful precisely because it invites readers to supply the emotion that the persona does not. This is the persona of the medieval Icelandic sagas, which inspired not only Ernest Hemingway but a whole generation of hard-boiled writers.

Third Person Omniscient

Third person omniscient ("all-knowing") gives you the most freedom to develop the story, and it works especially well in stories with complex plots or large settings where you must use multiple viewpoints to tell the story — for example, if you are skipping from Cape Canaveral to an orbiting shuttle to an alien spacecraft closing in on Earth.

Third person omniscient can, however, cause your reader to feel uncertain about whom to identify with in the story. If you are going to skip from one point of view to another, do so early in the story, before readers have fully identified with the original point of view. You'll drive your readers crazy if you spend 40 pages with one character and then kill him off before switching to some other character.

In third person omniscient, the author's persona can develop in any of several directions.

Episodically Limited

In episodically limited point of view, whoever is the point of view for a particular scene determines the persona. An elderly wizard sees and describes events from his particular point of view, while a teenage pickpocket does so quite differently. So the narrator, in a scene from the wizard's point of view, has a persona quite different from that of the pickpocket: a different vocabulary, a different set of values, a different set of priorities, even a difference in what he notices and fails to notice.

As a general rule, point of view should not change during a scene. So if a wizard is the point of view in a scene involving him and a pickpocket, the story shouldn't suddenly switch to the pickpocket's point of view until that scene is resolved and the story has moved on to another scene.

Occasional Interrupter

With an occasional interrupter, the author steps in from time to time to supply necessary information but otherwise stays in the background. The dialogue, thoughts, and behavior of the characters supply all other information readers need.

Editorial Commentator

The editorial commentator persona has a distinct attitude toward the story's characters and events, and frequently comments on them. The editorial commentator may be a character in the story, often with a name, but is usually at some distance from the main events; in some cases, there may even be an editorial commentator reporting the narrative of someone else about events involving still other people.

Since documents are often critical in SF and fantasy, the editorial commentator may literally be some kind of editor. Tolkien presents himself as the editor of much earlier documents relating the story of the War of the Ring. In Margaret Atwood's *The Handmaid's Tale,* the first person narrative of the hero, Offred, turns out to be the subject of scholarly discussion centuries later.

The editorial commentator is not always reliable; he or she may lie to us, or misunderstand the true significance of events. James De Mille uses this device very wittily in his 19th-century dystopia, *A Strange Manuscript Found in a Copper Cylinder.* Some educated men, becalmed in a yacht, are listening to one of their party reading the manuscript they've just retrieved from a floating copper cylinder. In between chapters of thud-and-blunder adventure, the listeners criticize the story's literary weaknesses, disarming our own criticism because the listeners are also clearly missing the point of the story.

HAZARDS OF USING PERSONA

The author's persona can influence your readers' reactions by helping readers feel close to or distant from the characters. Three major hazards are connected to use of the persona.

Sentimentality

One problem is when the author's editorial rhetoric tries to evoke an emotional response that the story's events cannot evoke by themselves — something like a cheerleader trying to win applause for a team that doesn't deserve it. This is a particular problem when using the editorial commentator persona. Dickens and other 19th-century novelists could get away with it, but that's precisely what makes them seem so dated nowadays.

Mannerism

Another hazard is when the author's persona seems more important than the story itself, and the author keeps reminding us of his or her presence through stylistic flamboyance, quirks of diction, or outright editorializing about the characters and events of the story.

You could write: "The sun was rising." But because you want to create a "poetic" mood, you write: "Rosy-fingered dawn was daubing the eastern horizon with lambent streamers of crimson, gold, and burnt orange." This is also a problem with the editorial commentator technique.

However, if the point of view is first person, and the narrator is a person given to stylistic flamboyance, quirks of diction, and so on, then the problem disappears; the persona is simply that of a rather egotistical individual who likes to show off. This was the approach I took in *Lifter,* my only SF novel written in first person, where the narrator is a smart-ass, "severely gifted" teenager who likes to show off his expressive ability.

Frigidity

The third problem is when the persona's excessive objectivity trivializes the events of the story, suggesting that the characters' problems need not be taken seriously. This is a particular hazard for hard-boiled fiction in the objective mode, whether first person or third person. If you and your characters don't seem to give a damn if someone gets killed, why should readers care? And if readers don't care, why should they read your story?

VERB TENSE

Verb tense can also affect the narrative style of the story. Most stories use the past tense: *I knocked on the door. She pulled out her dagger.* This is usually quite adequate although flashbacks can cause awkwardness: *I had knocked on the door. She had pulled out her dagger.* A little of that goes a long way.

Be careful to write consistently in one verb tense unless your narrator is a person who might switch tenses: *So I went to see my probation officer, and she tells me I can't hang out with my old buddies anymore.*

Some writers achieve a kind of immediacy through use of the present tense: *I knock on the door. She pulls out her dagger.* Readers don't feel anyone knows the outcome of events because they are occurring as they read, in "real time." Some writers also enjoy the present tense because it seems arty or avant-garde. But note that Dickens was using it in *Bleak House* in the 1850s! Most modern readers, at least of science fiction and fantasy, don't enjoy the present tense, so editors are often reluctant to let their authors use it.

I used present tense in my first novel, *The Empire of Time,* thinking it gave some sort of immediacy to the story. Instead it only delayed my editor's decision to buy it, and the offer was contingent on switching to past tense. I switched. And I've never switched back.

12

Exposition and Dialogue

My writing career didn't really begin until I got the best rejection letter of my life. Actually, my agent got the letter and sent it along to me. He'd submitted an early version of my novel *Icequake* to Judy-Lynn del Rey at Del Rey Books. She'd turned it down, but with a simple statement that made me finally get a grip on my writing.

"He's telling, not showing," she said. And I knew she was absolutely right. I sat down and rewrote *Icequake,* and the new version sold. Judy-Lynn didn't buy it, but she did buy *The Empire of Time;* Del Rey Books later published a whole string of my novels. By way of passing the favor forward, I want to show you — not tell you — what she meant.

SHOW OR TELL: WHICH IS BETTER?

Novice writers (and some professionals) often fall into the trap of "expositing" information instead of presenting it dramatically.

Sometimes exposition is inevitable, or even desirable. Lloyd Abbey, in his brilliant SF novel *The Last Whales,* gives us exactly one line of human dialogue; his characters, all being whales, can't speak to one another, so the narrator must tell us what they think and do. Gabriel García Márquez can also write superb exposition page after page.

Most of us ordinary mortals, however, need to dramatize our characters and their feelings. Otherwise our readers will tire of our editorials.

Consider the following expository and dramatic passages. Which more adequately conveys what the author is trying to show to readers?

> Colonel Vanessa Bridger was a career Starmarine: a tall woman of 34 with shoulder-length red hair and a pale complexion. She often lost her temper; when she did, her fair skin turned a deep pink, and she often swore. She was full of energy, and became impatient at even the slightest delay or impediment to her plans. Marshall Davidson, her logistics officer, was a balding, mild-mannered, nervous man of 44 who was often afraid of her. He was also annoyed with himself for letting her bully him. While he was a good administrator he had never seen combat, and Vanessa never let him forget it.

or

> Vanessa abruptly shot up from her desk. A shaft of sunlight from the window behind her seemed to strike fire from her long red hair as she shook her head violently.
>
> "No, Marshall! Goddamn it, this won't do! Didn't I make myself clear?"
>
> "Yes, C-Colonel Bridger, b-but-"
>
> "And you understood what I told you, didn't you?" Her pale skin was flushing pink, and Marshall saw the signs of a classic outburst on the way. She took a step toward him, forcing him to look up to meet her gaze; she must be a good four inches taller. He raised his hands in supplication,

then caught himself and tried to make the gesture look like the smoothing of hair he no longer had. He felt sweat on his bald scalp.

"Colonel, it was a—"

"It was another one of your screwups, Marshall! You're supposed to be the hotshot brigade logistician, but you don't seem to understand the first thing about what a combat unit needs when it goes into action. We're committed to a Thursday deadline. I'm going to make that damn deadline, whether or not you're here to help me. Now, am I going to get some cooperation from you, or not?"

Marshall nodded, cursing himself for his slavish obedience. Forty-four years old, and taking this abuse from a woman ten years younger. And she would rub it in that he'd never seen action. Rank or no rank, why didn't he just tell her to shove it?

"All the way, Colonel Bridger. We'll get right on it."

"Damn well better." Her voice softened; the pink faded from her cheeks. "Okay, dismissed."

A paragraph of exposition — easy to write but dull and unpersuasive — has turned into a scene: the portrayal of a conflict and its resolution. The scene has also prepared us for further scenes. Maybe Marshall's going to destroy himself for Vanessa, or poison her; maybe Vanessa's going to learn how to treat her staff better.

Most importantly, the authorial judgments in the exposition are now happening in the minds of the characters and the minds of readers who may well agree with Marshall, or side with Vanessa.

Here's another example:

Jerry was 19. Since leaving Paid Study a year before, he had done almost nothing. He had held a series of part-time jobs around the habitat, none of them lasting more than a few weeks. His girlfriend Judy, meanwhile, was holding down two jobs to help pay for her second year of college at

Copernicus Tech. Jerry controlled her with a combination of extroverted charm and bullying sulkiness. Secretly he envied her ambition and feared that she would leave him if he ever relaxed his grip on her.

or

"Hey, good-lookin'," Jerry said as he ambled into the coffee shop and took his usual booth by the screen. Earth and Luna were both crescents this week, bright even though the screen had stepped down the image.

"Hi," said Judy. She took out her order pad.

"Hey, I'm real sorry about what I said last night. I was way outta line."

"Would you like to order?"

"Hey, I said I was sorry, all right? Gimme a break."

"That's fine. But Murray says not to let my social life get in the way of my job. So you've got to order something for a change."

He snorted incredulously. "Hey, I'm broke, babe."

She stared at the screen. "You can't hang out here all day for the price of a cup of coffee, Jerry. Not anymore. Murray says he'll have to let me go if you do."

"Well, tell him to get stuffed."

"Jerry, be reasonable. I can't. I need … this … job."

"Hey, you already got the job at the lab."

"That's nights, and it hardly pays anything. I've got my whole second year at Copernicus to pay for in this vacation." She pointed at Luna's crescent on the screen. "You know what transport costs these days, even into a little gravity well like Luna's. Jerry, maybe we can talk about this after I get off work, okay?"

"Yeah, right. See you the day you leave for Luna, then."

"Jerry, don't. Okay? See you at four, okay?"

He got up, shrugging. "Yeah, sure. Guess I'll go home and watch holos until then." He glared at her. "Don't be too nice to the guys who come in here. I find out you been fooling around with anybody, you know you're in trouble, right?"

"Right, Jerry. I'm really sorry. See you later, okay?"

Again we have a conflict that promises to lead to further conflicts and their resolution. We want to know if Judy will ditch Jerry, or if Jerry will smarten up. Their relationship reveals itself through their dialogue, not through the author's editorializing. Her constant use of his name, and her nervous "Okay?" make her sound like a supplicant. No doubt, if she does ditch him or smarten him up, those mannerisms will vanish from her speech — and Jerry's speech will change too.

Note that both these examples involve a power struggle. Someone is determined to be the boss, to get his or her way. Most scenes present such a struggle: someone decides on pizza or hamburgers for dinner, someone decides the date for D-day, someone decides to jump from the pod to the air lock without a space suit. We as readers want to see the resources that go into the struggle: raw masculinity, clever technology, cynical intelligence, subtle sexual manipulation, political courage, suicidal desperation.

Depending on which resources win, we endorse one myth or another about the way the world operates: that raw masculinity always triumphs, that political courage leads nowhere, and so on. Of course, if we are writing ironically, we are rejecting the very myths we seem to support. By using raw macho bullying mixed with a little self-pity, Jerry seems to win his power struggle with Judy. But few readers would admire him for the way he does it, or expect him to succeed in the long term with such tactics. That's because your readers' myths probably teach them that a Real Man wouldn't behave that way — and a Real Woman wouldn't put up with it. (When I use the Jerry and Judy passage in my fiction-writing workshops, the women in the class are furious with Jerry — and almost as angry with Judy for putting up with him.)

Think carefully about this as you develop your scenes. As you dramatize a myth, you also test its limits. If your hero always wins arguments in a blaze of gunfire because Real Men Shoot Straight, he may become awfully tiresome awfully fast. If your hero keeps bursting into tears because Real Women Are Sensitive Creatures, your readers may want to hand her a hankie and tell her to grow up. Ideally, the power struggle in each scene should both tell us something new and surprising about the characters and hint at something still hiding beneath the surface of the myth — like the insecurity that underlies Jerry's and Vanessa's bullying.

"LET'S TALK ABOUT DIALOGUE," HE PONTIFICATED

Dialogue has to sound like speech, but it can't be a mere transcript; most people don't speak precisely or concisely enough to serve the writer's needs. Good dialogue has several functions:

- *To be expository:* to tell us, through the conversations of the characters, what we need to know to make sense of the story.

- *To convey character:* to show us what kinds of people we're dealing with.

- *To convey a sense of place and time:* to evoke the speech patterns, vocabulary, and rhythms of specific kinds of people.

- *To develop conflict:* to show how some people use language to dominate others, or fail to do so.

Each of these functions has its hazards. Expository dialogue can be dreadful:

> "We'll be in Vancouver in thirty minutes," the shuttle attendant said as the hyperjet roared up out of Singapore Spaceport. "It's the Canadian Republic's biggest West Coast city, with a population of almost seven million in the metropolitan area."

Dialogue can convey character, but the writer may bog down in chatter that doesn't advance the story.

"When I was a kid," said Julie, "I had a stuffed bear named Julius. He was a sweet old thing, and whenever I was upset I'd howl for him."

(Unless Julie is going to howl for Julius when her husband leaves her, this kind of remark is pointless.)

Dialogue that conveys a specific place and time can become exaggerated and stereotyped:

"Pretty hot ootside, eh?" remarked Sergeant Renfrew of the Royal Canadian Automated Police. "Good day to get oot of the hoose and oot on the saltchuck, eh? Catch us a couple of skookum salmon, eh?"

Dialogue that develops conflict has to do so while also being expository, portraying character, and staying true to the time and place:

"Gadzooks," said Thewbold the Barbarian as he dismounted from his war steed. "Knowest thou, my lady, that thou wast doing five leagues an hour in a three-league zone? Wouldst thou please present thy charioteer's license and registration?"

"Oh man, this really sucks," snarled Princess Sadistika as she drew the parchment scroll from her bag of needments.

To see how awful "real" dialogue is, dig up a copy of the Watergate Tapes transcripts. President Nixon and his henchmen were not only crooks, they could barely speak English. Your job as a dialogue writer is to convey character and move the story along, without bogging down in the repetitive mumbling that most people use.

Some tips for making your dialogue "better than real":

(a) Pay attention to generation tags — words or mannerisms that only people of a certain generation use. Like, Gen-Xers tend to finish a statement like it was a question? In a story set in the 21st century, this will be the way old folks talk, and you can invent your own tags for kids born circa 2025.

(b) Pay attention to locale tags — words or phrases specific to a region. "We were in a car smash" is Tennessee English; "We were in a fender bender" is California English for the same accident. "We had a few beers" is American; "We had a few beer, eh?" is Canadian. Imagine the slang of Australian colonists at the south pole of Mars, setting them off from the Second British Empire that dominates Earth in the 22nd century.

(c) Pay attention to class tags — terms that only peasants or clerks or aristocrats use. In your fantasy story, peasants might talk just in blunt Anglo-Saxon words, while aristocrats expostulate in exquisitely eloquent polysyllabic Greco-Latin terminology. (The aristocrats' middle-class clerks might speak even more elaborately, trying to imitate their masters.)

(d) Pay attention to shop talk — the in-group jargon of specialized professions. In his novel *Freeware,* Rudy Rucker uses an elaborate quasi-mathematical shop talk to explain the non-stop nonsense he's presenting. It's great fun (and a lovely parody of today's techno-nerd shop talk).

(e) Pay attention to speech rhythms. These can vary with class, generation, region, and nationality. If you live near the U.S.-Canada border, watch television newscasts from the other country and pay attention to the announcers' speech rhythms. Where do they stress a word, and where do they glide over it? If you can get the BBC World News, so much the better. You may notice that a Briton will say "I've a new computer," while an American will say, "I've got a new computer" — which changes the rhythm of the whole sentence.

(f) Minimize mannerisms. Don't give your hero's pal a stutter just to contrast his or her dialogue with the hero's. Don't let your hero say "Eew, gross" every time something bad happens. Be careful with dialects ("I say, old bean, care to join me in a spot of tea?"), especially if you're not utterly familiar with them as spoken languages.

(g) Read your dialogue out loud. Does it sound natural, as if real people might speak it under the conditions you describe? If not, rewrite.

Dialogue Hazards

Here are some dialogue hazards to avoid:

- Too much faithfulness to speech: "Um, uh, y'know, geez, well, like"

- Unusual spellings: use "Yeah," not "Yeh" or "Yea" or "Ya"

- Too much use of "he said," "she said"

- Too much variation: "he averred," "she riposted"

- Dialect exaggeration: "Lawsy, Miz Scahlut, us's wuhkin' jes' as fas' as us kin."

- Excessive direct address:

  "Tell me, Marshall, your opinion of Vanessa."

  "I hate her, Roger."

  "Why is that, Marshall?"

  "She bullies everyone, Roger."

Dialogue Style Conventions

Just as there are dialogue hazards to avoid, there are dialogue style conventions to consider:

- Each new speaker requires a new paragraph, properly indented and set off by quotation marks.

- "Use double quotations," Crawford advised, "and remember to place commas and periods inside those quotation marks." (While American publishers use double quotes for dialogue and single quotes within the quotation, British and most other Commonwealth publishers tend to do just the reverse. Canadian publishers, however, usually follow the American practice. See Chapter 14 for more on quotation marks.)

- "If a speaker goes on for more than one paragraph," the count responded in his heavy Transylvanian accent, "do not close off the quotation marks at the end of the first paragraph.

"Simply place quotation marks at the beginning of the next paragraph, and carry on to the end of the quotation."

Use "he said" expressions only when you must to avoid confusion about who's speaking. You can signal increasing tension by moving from "he said" to "he snapped," to "he snarled," to "he bellowed furiously." But the dialogue itself should convey that changing mood, and make such comments needless.

Action as well as speech is a part of dialogue. We expect to know when the speakers pause, where they're looking, what they're doing with their hands, how they respond to one another. The characters' speech becomes just one aspect of their interactions; sometimes their words are all we need, but sometimes we definitely need more.

This is especially true when you're trying to convey a conflict between what your characters say and what they feel: their nonverbal messages are going to be far more reliable than their spoken words.

Rely on rhythm and vocabulary, not phonetic spelling, to convey accent or dialect.

If you are giving us your characters' exact unspoken thoughts, use italics. If you are paraphrasing those thoughts, use regular roman type:

> *Now what does she want?* he asked himself. *Isn't she ever satisfied?*

> Marshall wondered what she wanted now. She was never satisfied.

If you plan to give readers a long passage of inner monologue, however, consider your readers' discomfort while having to read line after line of italic print.

To emphasize a word in a line of italic type, use roman type:

> *Isn't she* ever *satisfied?*

13

Symbolism
and All That

Maybe you never got anything out of your literature courses except a strong dislike for analyzing a story to death. Sometimes the symbolic interpretation of a story or poem can seem pretty farfetched.

Nevertheless, as soon as you start writing, you start writing on some kind of symbolic level. Some writers are very powerful symbolists, but don't realize it; that's why authors are often poor critics of their own work.

You may argue that your writing simply comes out of your own life and experience and has nothing to do with literary writing. Well, no doubt you'll include elements of your own life, but whether you like it or not, you'll find yourself treating that experience like gingerbread dough: You'll shape it into a mold to create a gingerbread figure, or you'll have a shapeless mess on your hands.

What you write is really a kind of commentary on everything you've read so far in your life. If you really get a kick out of fantasy novels, and you write one which you intend to be quite different from most fantasies, your novel is still a comment on what you've read — and on what you've done.

Symbolism in your writing will tend to reflect the kind of story you're writing. To paraphrase Northrop Frye very crudely, every story is about a search for identity. That identity depends largely on the protagonist's position (or lack of position) in society.

As mentioned in Chapter 9, a *tragic* story shows a person who moves from a socially integrated position (Hamlet, the Prince of Denmark; Oedipus, the King of Thebes) to a socially isolated or annihilated one (a dead prince, a blind beggar). Since most of us aren't as high in status, we watch in horror as a person who is a pillar of his or her society suddenly collapses and threatens to collapse the whole society as well.

We feel slightly reassured when we see that some fatal personal flaw (indecision, arrogance) leads to the hero's fall; if we are decisive, or modest, maybe we can avoid a similar disaster in our own lives.

A *comic* story shows a person moving from social isolation (symbolized by poverty, lack of recognition, and single status) to social integration (wealth, status, and marriage to one's beloved). Most of the laughs in comedy come from the challenge to the social order that arises when, for example, a young and foolish boy wants to marry a rich girl against her father's wishes. Since most of us feel like outsiders, we identify with the boy and the girl and hope that they overthrow the status quo.

Fiction in the Western tradition draws on two major sources: ancient Greek literature and the Judeo-Christian Bible. Both sources are concerned with preservation or restoration of society and with the individual hero as savior or social redeemer. Hamlet wants to redeem Denmark from his uncle's usurpation; Oedipus wants to save Thebes from the curse that he himself unintentionally placed on it.

In precisely the same way, the private eye redeems his or her society by identifying who is guilty (and therefore who is innocent); the frontier gunman risks his life to preserve the honest pioneers; the mutant telepath faces danger to search for fellow mutants; the fugitive princess battles the tyrannical usurper to retrieve her throne and rescue her people.

Now, you can play this straight or you can twist it. If you play it straight, your hero is moving from isolation to integration (though often, like Moses and the typical private eye, he or she leads others to the promised land but can't enter it himself or herself). You're telling a comic story, with a happy ending.

But you may decide to twist this formula into an ironic one. The private eye may find that everyone is guilty. The gunman may be in the pay of crooked land speculators. The mutant may find he is sterile, that his talents will die with him. As noted in Chapter 9, an ironic plot undercuts its surface meaning. Winston Smith, in *Nineteen Eighty-Four,* is happily integrated at the end of the story, but we don't share his happiness. We just feel a kind of nauseated pity for him. That's because in an ironic story, we understand the characters and their predicament better than they themselves do.

Northrop Frye argues that fiction has two structural principles. The first is a struggle between ideal and demonic worlds, the world as we wish it were and the world as we wish it weren't. The second principle is the natural cycle: day into night, spring into summer. We express these principles with symbols — angels and devils, fire and ice, maidens and crones, gardens and deserts. How you use symbols can also undercut or change your apparent meaning. Let's take a look at some common symbols and patterns, and how they can comment on your story.

THE NATURAL CYCLE

Day to night, winter to spring, youth to old age. These suggest all kinds of imagery:

Light = goodness; Darkness = evil

Winter = despair; Spring = hope

Girl = innocence; Crone = evil knowledge, impending death

Frye argues that we associate images of spring with comedy; images of summer with romance; images of autumn with tragedy; images of winter with satire and irony. Note, however, that here *comedy* means a story of social unification; *tragedy* means a story of social isolation; and *romance* means a story in which the characters are larger than life and encounter wonders usually not seen in reality. Such a romance may be comic or tragic (or both — *The Lord of the Rings* is comic, but many of its characters suffer death or bitter isolation in their efforts to save Middle Earth).

Bear in mind that images associated with these cycles are usually all you need: at the end of *Nineteen Eighty-Four,* a cold April wind kills the crocuses that ought to promise hope and renewal. Similarly, autumn leaves can symbolize an aging person, a dying society, or the onset of evil.

THE NATURAL VERSUS THE HUMAN WORLD

Desert versus garden, sinister forest versus park: A hostile natural world versus a world designed for human benefit and happiness. (*Desert* doesn't mean "dry and sandy," but "deserted, empty of humanity" — and therefore hostile.)

Pastoral world versus city: Childlike humanity in harmony with nature; adult humanity in an entirely artificial environment.

In Western literature, the journey from innocence to experience is often symbolized by the protagonist's journey from an idyllic world close to nature, to an urban world that has closed itself against nature. (In biblical terms, this is the journey from Eden, through the desert of the fallen world, to the Heavenly City.) Returns to the natural world are sometimes successful, and sometimes the protagonist manages to bring the urban world into a new harmony with nature. In other cases, an urban hero finds meaning and value through some kind of contact with nature.

THE HERO'S QUEST

No literary hero ever succeeded by staying home. A dangerous journey is the only way heroes can test themselves, affirm their identity, and rescue (or fail to rescue) their society.

The quest really begins at birth, and goes through some familiar stages. Since we see the same stages even in ancient mythology, they seem to be deeply ingrained in our minds as the way we all achieve our identity. In modern fiction, however, we may treat the quest somewhat ironically, and the hero doesn't have to go through all the stages.

Is the quest the same for a female hero as it is for a male hero? Increasingly the answer is yes. Traditionally, the female was just a symbol of the hero's success: "getting the girl" meant winning. But in both SF and fantasy, women's roles have changed. They are commanding interstellar warships, leading revolts against tyrants, and saving their societies. Walter Jon Williams's urban fantasies, *Metropolitan* and *City on Fire,* give us a female hero who transcends her humble origins and guides a world-transforming revolution. The hero in S. M. Stirling's *Island in the Sea of Time* is a black lesbian Coast Guard captain skilled in Japanese martial arts.

Whether attention falls more on the male or on the female, success means the formation of a new society, symbolized by the union of lovers. Typically these are male and female, but lesbian or gay unions are not out of the question.

THE TEN STAGES OF THE HERO'S QUEST

Stage 1: Mysterious or unusual birth (Jupiter, Oedipus, Jesus, King Arthur, Odd John, Superman).

Stage 2: Prophecy that the hero will overthrow the present order, and/or restore a vanished order (Moses, Oedipus, Jesus, Aragorn).

Stage 3: Threat from a monstrous or false father (Saturn versus Jupiter, Herod versus Jesus, Darth Vader versus Luke Skywalker).

Stage 4: Secluded childhood among humble people in a pastoral setting (Oedipus among the shepherds, Frodo Baggins in the Shire, Luke Skywalker on Tattooine).

Stage 5: Signs of the hero's unusual nature — not always positive (Hercules strangling serpents in his cradle, "Odd John" Wainwright's rapid acquisition of language and mathematics and his murder of a policeman). At this point the hero is something of an outsider, often looked down upon or even feared.

Stage 6: Journey/quest. Some person or event impels the hero to leave home on an urgent mission — often after rejecting the mission twice, the hero accepts it on the third demand. This leads to a series of adventures and ordeals (usually with a band of companions) that test the hero's virtues and skills: physical and moral courage, loyalty, dedication, and so forth (Moses and the Jews in the wilderness, Odysseus wandering the world, Frodo and Sam's journey to Mordor).

Stage 7: The confrontation. The quest often ends in a climactic struggle with a monstrous or false version of the hero: an evil brother or oppressive father (Frodo versus Gollum, Ged versus his shadow in *Wizard of Earthsea,* Luke Skywalker versus Darth Vader).

Stage 8: Death — real or symbolic. The hero may literally die and enter the afterlife (Jesus harrowing Hell), or the hero may experience a purely symbolic death, often by going underground (Huck Finn and Tom Sawyer in the cavern).

Stage 9: Rebirth. The hero returns to the world, often greatly changed (Frodo back from Mordor).

Stage 10: Recognition as savior/king; formation of new society around him (Frodo scouring the Shire).

Obviously not every story follows these ten stages, but our familiarity with the hero's quest forms a kind of script that prepares us for any particular version of it.

In ironic stories, the hero's quest turns into a kind of parody. In my novel *Eyas,* for example, the orphaned prince Brightspear experiences a classic hero's upbringing and quest, but he's the villain of the story. Most of his adventures and triumphs are offstage, including the regaining of his father's throne. In effect, he succeeds as a parody-hero until he confronts the novel's true hero, Eyas. Each of them is the evil brother of the other.

SYMBOLIC IMAGES

A symbol may be good or evil, depending on its context, and the writer is quite free to develop the context to convey a particular symbolism. For example, the tree is usually a symbol of life — but not if you use it as the venue for a lynching, or you turn its wood into a crucifix or a gibbet. Here are some images and their most common symbolic meanings:

- *Garden:* nature ordered to serve human needs (*paradise* comes from a Persian word for garden)

- *Wilderness, desert:* nature hostile to human needs

- *River:* life, often seen as ending in death as the river ends in the sea

- *Sea:* chaos, death; source of life

- *Flower:* youth, sexuality; red flowers symbolize death of young men

- *Pastoral animals:* ordered human society

- *Predatory animals:* evil; threats to human order

- *Fire:* light and life or hell and lust

- *Sky:* heaven; fate or necessity

- *Bridge:* link between worlds, between life and death

SYMBOLIC CHARACTERS

Different types of characters recur so often that they've become archetypes and have acquired their own names. Here are some of the most common:

- *Eiron:* one who deprecates himself and appears less than he really is; includes most types of hero (Ulysses, Frodo, Huck Finn). The term "irony" derives from this Greek term "eiron."

- *Alazon:* an impostor, one who boasts and presents himself or herself as more than he or she really is; subtypes include the braggart soldier (General Buck Turgidson in the movie *Dr. Strangelove*) and obsessed philosopher/mad scientist (Saruman, and Dr. Strangelove himself). "Alazon" is another term from Greek comedy, and in my novel *Tsunami,* I named my villain "Allison"; although he starts as a movie director, he ends up as a braggart soldier.

- *Tricky slave:* the hero's helper (Jim in *The Adventures of Huckleberry Finn;* Gollum in *The Lord of the Rings*).

- *Helpful giant:* the hero's helper; in tune with nature (Ents in *The Lord of the Rings;* Chewbacca in *Star Wars*).

- *Wise old man:* the hero's helper; possessor of knowledge (Tolkien's Gandalf, Obi-Wan Kenobi in *Star Wars*).

- *Buffoon:* creates a festive mood, relieves tension (Sam Gamgee in *The Lord of the Rings,* Mercutio in *Romeo and Juliet*).

- *Churl:* straight man, killjoy, or bumpkin (Uriah Heep in *David Copperfield*).

- *Fair maiden:* symbol of purity and redemption (Rowena in Sir Walter Scott's *Ivanhoe*) or of repressed sexuality.

- *Dark woman:* symbol of lust and temptation (the Jewish Rebecca in *Ivanhoe*) or of natural sexuality.

- *Hero's double:* represents the dark side of the hero's character (Ged's shadow in Le Guin's *Wizard of Earthsea*).

Since these images are much older than what is now politically correct, they can cause problems; some readers may see them as affirmations of old, oppressive social values. However, many modern writers now use them ironically to criticize, not endorse, the values the images originally expressed. Nevertheless, be aware that if your female heroes are always blonde virgins and your female villains are always seductive brunettes, you may be sending a message you don't consciously intend.

DEVELOPING YOUR OWN SYMBOLS

Be aware also that you're perfectly free to develop your own symbolic system. Just as the Rosebud sled in *Citizen Kane* symbolizes Kane's lost childhood innocence, you can make a symbol out of a hat rack, a catcher's mitt, or an old bus schedule. You're also free to make your symbols understandable to your readers, or to keep them part of your private mythology. If you associate a catcher's mitt with the death of your hero's father, readers will understand — on some level — what you're trying to say. If the catcher's mitt seems important to your hero, but you don't tell us why, we can only guess at the symbolic meaning.

Don't try too self-consciously to be symbolic. But if certain images, objects, or events seem to dominate your thinking about your novel, write yourself a letter about them. See whether they might indeed carry some symbolic level of meaning, and if that level is in harmony with your conscious intent.

As we wrap up this section on the craft of writing, use Checklist 1 to ensure that your writing style is as powerful as it can be.

CHECKLIST I
STYLE FOR FICTION WRITERS

As you begin to develop your outline, and then the actual text of your novel, you can save time and energy by making sure that your writing style requires virtually no copyediting.

In the narrative:

❑ Do any sentences begin with the words "There" or "It"? They can almost certainly benefit from revision. (Compare: "There were three swordsmen who had sworn to kill him." "Three swordsmen had sworn to kill him.")

❑ Are you using passive voice instead of active voice? (Compare: "Is passive voice being used?") Put it in active voice!

❑ Are you repeating what you've already told your readers? Are you telegraphing your punches?

❑ Are you using trite phrases, clichés, or deliberately unusual words? You'd better have a very good reason for doing so.

❑ Are you terse? Or, alternatively, are you expressing your thoughts with a perhaps excessive plethora of gratuitous and surplus verbiage, whose predictably foreseeable consequences, needless to say, include a somewhat repetitious redundancy?

❑ Are you grammatically correct? Are spelling and punctuation correct? (This is not mere detail work, but basic craft.)

❑ Is the prose fluent and varied in rhythm, and is the tone suitable to the type of story you're telling?

❑ Are you as narrator intruding on the story through witticisms, editorializing, or self-consciously "fine" writing?

In the dialogue:

❑ Are you punctuating dialogue correctly, so that you neither confuse nor distract your readers?

❑ Are your characters speaking naturally, as they would in reality, but more coherently?

❑ Does every line of dialogue advance the story, revealing something new about the plot or the characters? If not, what is its justification?

❑ Are your characters so distinct in their speech—in diction, rhythm, and mannerism—that you rarely need to add "he said" or "she said"?

Part 3:
Getting Published

14

The Mechanics of Manuscript Production

Getting a manuscript into final shape is a lot of work for you as an author, and more work for your editor. First let's see how you can save work for yourself while you're writing; then we'll look at making life easier for your editor.

EXPLOITING YOUR WORD PROCESSOR

Creating a consistent, readable manuscript isn't the chore that it used to be. Computers have made creation and revision far easier, and even the clumsiest word processor is far superior to even the best typewriter. Here are some suggestions for exploiting your word processor's effectiveness in generating a manuscript.

Set Up a Template

A template is a blank file with all the formatting set up as you want it: margin widths, fonts, paragraph indents, page numbers, and so on. You may also choose to modify the defaults in your word processor, so that every new file you start up has all your preferred formatting.

Many writers like to put each chapter or short story in a file of its own. All you need to do is open up your template, name the new file it creates, and get to work. If you number your chapters, you may wish to name the files Chapter 01, Chapter 02, because of how many operating systems alphabetize files. That is, it usually puts Chapters 10 and 11 immediately after Chapter 1 in your directory or folder, and it will be harder for you to navigate at a glance.

Or you can choose to keep the whole story in a single huge file. The advantage to this is being able to quickly skip around your manuscript — and word counts, pagination, and search-and-replace chores are much easier.

Don't Decorate the Page

A frame around the text, an unusual font, dingbats, and clip art are all temptations to avoid. They are distractions to the editor. Your decorations won't appear in the printed book, so why clutter the manuscript with them?

Minimize the fonts and styles of type you use in your manuscript. All you really need is a roman typeface like this, and *an italic typeface like this*. (Some publishers don't even like italics; they'd rather you underline anything that you want to see in italic.)

Make On-Screen Reading Easier for Yourself

Computer monitors are reader-hostile. Reading speed falls by up to 25 percent when we read off the monitor, and proofreading accuracy drops very quickly. Most of the fonts on your computer may look sharp when you print them out, but they can be murder to read on-screen.

For writing, I suggest you use a font specifically designed for on-screen reading. Two good fonts are Times New Roman and Georgia.

Even at 12 points, they're big and clear — especially Georgia. At 14 points, they're even better (in typesetting, a point is about one-72nd of an inch). You should experiment to find the right type size for the font you prefer.

However, you may prefer to print out the final manuscript in some other font and size, which can mean minor formatting discrepancies like inconsistent page numbers. (Think about printing out your proofreading drafts in a font that you rarely use, a font that is unfamiliar but still readable, of course. This will help you read your own text as a stranger would, so you'll catch mistakes more easily and consistently.)

I suggest you double-space your text when you're writing, even if it means more scrolling. You'll double-space when you print out the manuscript to make reading easy for your editor; make it easy for yourself as well, both on screen and on paper. (Expect to print out at least one draft of the manuscript for proofreading and editing before the printout you create for your editor.)

You may even want to compose different drafts in different fonts. For this book, I've used Georgia for the first draft; after a revision I've switched the font to Book Antiqua. That way I can tell at a glance which draft I'm looking at.

Text is also easier to read in a *serif* font than in a *sans serif* font. The little hooks and feet on serif fonts seem to carry the eye along line after line. That's why most books and periodicals use serif fonts, reserving sans serif for headlines and short passages.

Keep Paragraphs Intact

Keeping paragraphs intact on the printed page means setting your template so that when a paragraph splits between pages one and two, the whole paragraph moves to page two. Sometimes this creates awkwardly high margins at the page bottom, but that's preferable to breaking the paragraph.

Avoid Elaborate Headers and Footers

The only purpose for putting your name and the story's title on every page is in case part of the manuscript gets separated from the rest. In that unlikely event, your last name should be enough to identify it.

Use the Search-and-Replace Feature

I once found I'd used a well-known person's name for a minor character in one of my early novels. That meant I had to go through the typescript searching for every mention and changing it. Talk about boring! Now you can do such chores in seconds. But be careful how you frame the command — if you change your hero's name from Bill to Bob, you may find that instead of paying his bills, Bob is paying his bobs.

Navigate Your Manuscript

Most word processors have "go to" features as well as commands to take you to the very beginning or end of a given file. In some cases, you can create bookmarks that you can jump to, just as you can on many websites. Jumping is a lot faster than scrolling.

Split Your Screen

In many cases you will need to refer to passages earlier in the file; if your word processor permits screen-splitting, you can simultaneously write while checking what you've written before.

Use Macros

If you have characters with long names, or you're getting tired of writing "Thewbold said," create a macro that will automatically produce the desired name or expression with a couple of keystrokes.

Or use search and replace: type "Thsa" while you're writing, and then go back and replace each example with "Thewbold said."

Use Computer Spelling Checkers and Grammar Checkers Suspiciously

Spelling checkers are notoriously dumb. They can't distinguish between "their," "there," and "they're." No spelling checker can replace a careful human. But current word processors often flag typos even as you work, enabling you to correct them on the fly. (Some will automatically correct common errors or words that you add to a correction list — if you type "edcuation," for example, such word processors will correct the spelling as soon as you hit the space bar.)

Bear in mind that the spellings your spelling checker approves may be considered wrong by the standards of your publisher's country. If you set your word processor's "language" to Canadian English, it will follow U.K. usage like "colour" and "standardise," which will only make more work for your long-suffering American editor. In such cases, add the more acceptable usage to your spelling checker's dictionary. You should also add any unusual names, so the spelling checker won't drive you crazy with repeated queries about Thewbold or Sadistika.

Grammar checkers are usually slow and annoying in their pickiness. At best they may alert you to bad habits, like overusing passive voice or creating strings of prepositional phrases.

How Readable Are You?

Grammar checkers often include one useful feature, however: a readability scale. By counting the number of syllables per word, and the number of words per sentence, your grammar checker can give you a rough estimate of the years of education your readers must have to make sense of your text. A student in grade 10 would therefore presumably have trouble with text whose readability scale puts it at grade 14, that is, second-year university. In actual fact, a grade 10 student might do very well with "difficult" writing, or might be lost with material on a grade 6 readability level. So don't take readability scales as infallible — only as general indicators of how large an audience you can expect to reach easily.

However, if you're consistently scoring grade 13 or 14, your sentences are probably longer and more polysyllabic than they need to be. Anywhere from grade 5 to grade 10 should be enough. You won't be dumbing down your text, just keeping it short and sweet. You can also try out your text at Readability.net (www.readability.net), where you can upload a Word file and get several different assessments.

Short sentences using short words may look as if they belong in a children's picture book, but if your content is solid you won't be dumbing it down. As Winston Churchill pointed out, "Big men use little words, and little men use big words" (11 words, 13 syllables). He wouldn't have sounded any smarter if he'd written: "Male individuals of unusually great moral character employ minuscule linguistic units, whereas males of contemptible personality resort at all opportunities to orotund verbiage." (23 words, 58 syllables).

If you break some of your long sentences into short ones, you'll see two benefits: the shorter sentences will have more impact, and so will the remaining long ones.

Use Word Count as a Motivator

Open a new chapter, bang away at it for a while, and count your words. If you write 250 words in 30 minutes, for example, you'll be motivated to keep going — every hour puts you 500 words closer to a complete manuscript. Keep a log, listing the word count for each chapter and a total for the whole manuscript. If you find you're adding 1,000 words every day, or even 250, the story becomes a project with a predictable finish date.

No doubt you've already developed some useful shortcuts and productivity habits. But don't sidetrack yourself by trying to master every aspect of your word processor. The goal, after all, is to produce a completed manuscript ready for market in the shortest time possible — not to qualify as a computer whiz.

BACK UP YOUR FILES

Don't ever forget to back up those files! And keep updated copies of these backups so you won't waste months or years of work if the computer's hard drive crashes or someone steals your computer — including your notes, log, correspondence, and research materials. Unless you have serious reasons for keeping earlier drafts, make sure that every copy, whether on your hard drive or on discs, is completely up to date.

BASIC MANUSCRIPT COPYEDITING PRINCIPLES

To you, your completed manuscript is a satisfyingly thick monument to your imagination, dedication, and storytelling genius. But as I mentioned, your editor is reading you as work, not as entertainment, and you owe her a manuscript that's as easy to work with as you can make it.

Maybe you're such a great storyteller that your editor won't care about the lousy spelling, the hit-or-miss grammar, the persistent misuse of quotation marks in dialogue. You wouldn't be the first. An editor once told me that one of his best-selling authors was a functional illiterate whose manuscripts required painfully detailed copyediting. Cleaning up this author's writing was such a chore that, once promoted to a senior position, the editor excused himself from ever copyediting this author again.

But if you're not that great a storyteller (or you just have a lot of self-respect), you should make it a matter of personal pride to deliver a manuscript that requires minimal copyediting. (See my essay on the CD about "pre-editing.")

For detailed advice on grammar and usage, you can buy and use any number of helpful references. What follows here is the least you need to know.

Punctuation

Quotation Marks

If you are submitting your manuscript to a Canadian or American publisher, use double quotation marks around dialogue and single quotation marks for quotes within quotes or words that the speaker is using in some special sense:

> "Looks like trouble," said Thewbold.
> "'Looks like trouble,'" Princess Sadistika mocked him. "What does a thick-skulled barbarian know of 'trouble'?"

Commas

If you're going to add an expression like "said Thewbold" at the end of a complete sentence in dialogue, insert a comma before the end quotation marks:

> "Shut up," Thewbold explained.

If your expression falls in the middle of a sentence in dialogue, set off the expression with commas before and after:

> "Shut up," said Thewbold, "or my broadsword will cleave you asunder."

Don't put a single comma between your subject and your verb:

> *Wrong:* The treacherous but beautiful Princess Sadistika, smiled sweetly at Thewbold.

If you insert a parenthetical phrase between subject and verb, put commas on both sides:

> Princess Sadistika, treacherous but beautiful, smiled sweetly at Thewbold.

But if you start with the phrase, use only one comma:

> Treacherous but beautiful, Princess Sadistika smiled sweetly at Thewbold.

If you have a long introductory phrase (five words or more), insert a comma before the main part of the sentence begins:

From a musty tomb of the Evil Ones, Thewbold had stolen a ruby talisman.

If the introductory phrase contains a verb, insert a comma no matter how short the phrase:

By stealing the talisman, Thewbold drew the attention of Princess Sadistika.

Running for the drawbridge, Thewbold drew the attention of the guards.

If you begin the sentence with a subordinate clause, always insert a comma before the main clause begins:

While Thewbold had known many women, none compared with Princess Sadistika.

Semicolons

Use a semicolon when you want to put together two main clauses (each with a subject and verb) to form a single sentence without using a conjunction. The semicolon signals that what follows it will be closely related to the first main clause:

Thewbold had known many women; none compared with Princess Sadistika.

Note: A comma after "women" would turn the above into a run-on sentence, giving your long-suffering editor more work.

Colons

Use a colon when you want to signal that what follows will explain or illustrate what you've just told readers:

He had angered the Evil Ones: eldritch beings born in an elder age.

In the doorway stood his foe: Baron Hamfist.

If you introduce a list, don't use a colon unless the sentence is grammatically complete before you begin the list.

Wrong: She loved: Thewbold, Ironbrow, Crushbone, and Hardnose.

Right: She loved many men: Thewbold, Ironbrow, Crushbone, and Hardnose.

You may also use a colon instead of a comma to introduce dialogue:

Sadistika spoke coldly: "You bore me, barbarian."

End Punctuation

A single period normally ends a declarative sentence, even if it ends in an abbreviation:

Evidently the spacecraft had crashed in Mesopotamia in 525 B.C.

When you end a sentence of dialogue, put the period or question mark inside the quotation marks:

"The air lock is open."
"Who opened it?"

But if the question mark does not belong to the quote, it should follow the closing quotation mark:

Did the captain understand what was meant by "The airlock is open"?

Don't use a question mark when you're really making a statement, not asking a question:

He wondered who had opened the air lock.

Use an exclamation mark (just one at a time) only in dialogue:

"The aliens opened the air lock, you idiot!"

In narrative, the exclamation mark looks like an attempt to whip up excitement. It also draws attention to you as the author, editorializing about your own story. But if you are reporting the agitated thoughts of your character, it's acceptable:

Murphy suddenly understood. The aliens had opened the air lock!

Capitalization

Proper Names

Whether it's a human or alien name — John Carter or Tars Tarkas — it takes capital letters. The same is true for place names: Cimmeria, Aquilonia, Earth, Terra. But don't capitalize names of elements, compounds, alloys, etc., unless they're brand names: small-v vanadium, capital-V Velcro.

Languages and nationalities usually take capital letters: English, Uruguayan, Kurdish, Esperanto. Races may or may not be capitalized: people may be black or Black, caucasian or Caucasian, but white people don't take a capital W and Asians always take a capital A. (If we were rational about this, life would be much happier.)

General practice suggests that an intelligent inhabitant of another planet or solar system deserves a capital letter: Martian, Jovian, Capellan. But other organisms or objects belonging to a planet should be in lowercase: the martian landscape, jovian bacteria.

Our own world poses capitalization problems: it's Earth or the earth (and sometimes Terra or Gaia), orbited by the Moon, the moon, or Luna. To my knowledge, no one has yet written a science fiction story in which people routinely refer to this planet as *Shijie* — the Chinese term for Earth.

Titles

When a title precedes a proper name, it takes a capital letter. When it follows a proper name, it's usually in lowercase:

> I learned that Lieutenant Simon Chang was a Royal Starmarine.

> I learned that Simon Chang was a lieutenant in the Royal Starmarines.

Directions don't take capital letters unless they're part of a proper name or refer to a general region:

> The probe glided west until it crashed in South Dakota.

The *Los Angeles Times* website showed a single stark head-line: Huge Quake Strikes Southland.

Capitals in Dialogue

Usually, any complete sentence in quotation marks will start with a capital letter, even if the sentence is part of a larger one:

> Thewbold unrolled the scroll and saw letters of writhing flame that said, "Cursed is he who reads these words."

Grammar

If you need detailed advice on grammar, a good course is the place to get it. But I can offer some reminders.

Subject-Verb Disagreement

If your subject is singular, then your verb has to be singular also:

> The dune crawler was stalled halfway up the road from the floor of Valles Marineris.

A plural or compound subject needs a plural verb:

> Two dune crawlers were lost in the avalanche.
> Chavez and Chang were the only survivors of the attack.

Be careful not to treat compound subjects as if they were singular:

> *Wrong:* Rain and hail was falling heavily on the mountain path.

> *Right:* Rain and hail were falling heavily on the mountain path.

In some cases, you can treat plurals as if they were single units:

> "Six years is a long time in suspended animation," Chang said. "And three million dollars is good pay for sleeping," Chavez replied.

Verb Tense

Most of your narrative will be in the simple past tense:

> He drew his saber.
> She smiled sweetly.

In some cases, however, you have to refer to a still earlier time than the moment you're describing. You're then using the past perfect tense:

> He had drawn his saber.
> She had smiled sweetly.

This can become a problem in long passages. Suppose you start with a chapter showing your hero in the year 2230, and then flash back in Chapter 2 to his boyhood in 2218? A whole chapter in past perfect (he had asked/she had complained/his mother had not believed him …) would be pretty wearisome.

One solution: date the chapters so readers will understand that they're jumping around in time, and then in each chapter use simple past tense. Another solution: start the chapter in past perfect and then switch back to simple perfect after a few sentences. It's awkward, but most readers will accept it.

Your characters' conversation doesn't have to be so grammatically pure. In speech we often switch verb tense in midsentence and neither we nor our listeners even notice:

> So I caught the Vancouver shuttle with 30 seconds to spare and the attendant says, "Please strap yourself in, sir."

In dialogue and some kinds of first person narrative, this sort of tense switching is perfectly okay. If your first person narrator is highly informal (or poorly educated), it would be out of character to use correct verb tense.

Misplaced Modifiers

Sometimes you may sabotage yourself by using a phrase in a way that's confusing or even unintentionally funny. For example:

> *Wrong:* Circling the planet, Jupiter loomed enormous in the ship's viewscreens.

Grammatically this means Jupiter, not the ship, was circling the planet. A phrase like "circling the planet" must refer to the subject of the sentence, so the subject has to be what or who is doing the circling:

> *Right:* Circling the planet, the crew saw Jupiter looming enormous in the ship's viewscreens.

Or you could change the phrase into a subordinate clause and write:

> As they circled the planet, the crew saw Jupiter looming enormous in the ship's viewscreens.

A misplaced modifier can be grammatically okay but still make the sentence unclear:

> The computer predicted in May the asteroid would strike Earth.

Does this mean the computer predicted it last May, or that the asteroid is due to arrive next May?

> A cyborg leased to Manjit Singh as a domestic servant was found shocked to death in her apartment by officers of the Deimopolis Constabulary.

Does this mean the constables killed a valuable cyborg, or that they discovered the cyborg's corpse? And was it Manjit Singh's apartment, or the cyborg's? Make it clear:

> Officers of the Deimopolis Constabulary discovered a cyborg, shocked to death, in the apartment of Manjit Singh; she had been leasing it as a domestic servant.

If you're really feeling uncertain about your basic language skills, treat English, or whatever language you're writing in, as just something else to research. If you had to know about waste-recycling problems in a space habitat, you'd study the topic and learn what you need. The same is true of grammar and word usage; and since you'll be applying your new knowledge all the time, it's likely to stick with you. Use Checklist 2 as a reminder of some basic copyediting principles.

CHECKLIST 2
COPYEDITING

This is not mere detail work, but basic craft. Learn standard English or forget about writing novels.

1. Are you grammatically correct?

No subject-verb disagreements

   ✗ Three amulets made by Gnarlfist was hidden in the tomb.

   ✔ Three amulets made by Gnarlfist were hidden in the tomb.

No run-on sentences

   ✗ Three amulets were hidden in the tomb, two others had been lost centuries earlier.

   ✔ Three amulets were hidden in the tomb; two others had been lost centuries earlier.

No sentence fragments

   ✗ Three amulets in the tomb.

   ✔ Three amulets were hidden in the tomb.

No dangling modifiers

   ✗ Glancing around the crypt, the sarcophagus was the only hiding place Thewbold could see. [*This means the sarcophagus was glancing around the crypt.*]

   ✔ Glancing around the crypt, Thewbold saw no hiding place but the sarcophagus.

2. Is verb tense consistent?

   ✔ Thewbold strode across the crypt. Then he pulls open the sarcophagus.

   ✗ Thewbold strode across the crypt. Then he pulled open the sarcophagus.

3. Are spelling and punctuation correct?

4. Are you punctuating dialogue correctly, so that you neither confuse nor distract your readers?

5. Are you indenting for a new paragraph each time a different character speaks?

> "Good morning, Skipper," Hanson said. "I hope you slept well."
>
> "Very well, Mr. Hanson. What's our ETA for lunar orbit?"
>
> "Three hours and twelve minutes, sir."

6. Are names and capitalizations consistent and correct? For example, a title before a name takes a capital (Lieutenant Hanson), but not after a name (Hanson was a new lieutenant). If you change Hanson's name to Hansen (or Fujimura), be sure to do a global search and replace to catch all uses of the name.

MANUSCRIPT FORMAT

Once your book appears in print, your publisher may return your manuscript as "dead matter." At that point it's of interest only to future PhD candidates — that is, if you become really famous. But when it first arrives in the publisher's office, it ought to look as inviting, clean, and professional as you can make it.

You want to make sure it's as readable (and correctable) as possible; don't give the editor an excuse to reject your manuscript because you make her eyes hurt and because she can't even find room to insert proper spelling and editorial comments.

Ideally, you'll submit your manuscript in laser-printed form. If you can't afford that, then use an inkjet printer (used with good bond paper, it's almost as good as laser). You might even take your manuscript on diskette to a local print shop.

Consider your choice of font. **A sans serif font like this is legible but not readable** — that is, you can recognize a word or phrase quickly, but reading page after page is exhausting. **A boldface font like this is even worse.** A serif font like this is more readable, so by all means choose one for the body of your manuscript text.

Point size is also important. As I mentioned earlier in this chapter, some fonts are very readable at 12 points, while others look minuscule. A serif font like Times New Roman is adequate at 12 points but better at 14.

Some people think the only font to use for submitting a manuscript is the monospace font Courier, `which looks like this` — very much like a typewriter. It has been suggested that with this font editors could better estimate word count. Well, that's what word processors are for! After witnessing one noisy debate about this issue in an online newsgroup for writers, I called my own publishers, to whom I'd been sending manuscripts in a variety of fonts (but not Courier). Which font did Del Rey Books prefer? The woman who answered my inquiry clearly thought I was crazy; as long as it was readable, Del Rey didn't care.

Paper should be standard 8½-by-11-inch, 20-pound white bond. Give yourself a margin of at least an inch top and bottom, and an inch or an inch and a half on the sides. Double-space your text. Do not put an extra double-space between paragraphs, unless you want a similar gap on the printed page to indicate a change of scene or passage of time.

Indent each paragraph about half an inch. A single space after a period is enough; double spaces are a relic of the past. And a single space should follow every comma, semicolon, and colon.

Use an em dash (—) with no spaces between the dash and the surrounding words (although some publishers prefer to set em dashes with spaces). Two hyphens (--) are an acceptable substitute. Underline text only if you cannot *italicize* it. Use "smart quotes," which curve, rather than "dumb quotes," which don't. Most word processors give you a choice.

Do not use a right-justified margin like this book! It may look tidy, but it creates gaps between words that make reading hard. (Publishers used advanced software that lets them control word spaces; your word processor can't do that.)

Avoid hyphenations. Also avoid widows and orphans — that is, a paragraph that begins on the last line of a page, or a paragraph that ends on the first line of the following page. Most word processors can kick such paragraphs onto the next page. This may create tall lower margins, but it's better than breaking a paragraph.

Be sure that each page displays a plain Arabic numeral in the upper or lower right-hand corner. Otherwise, don't bother with a header or footer.

Chances are that if a publisher accepts your novel, you'll have to supply an electronic copy of the manuscript as well as one on paper. Be sure to make it a copy the publisher's computers can read. It's not really a big problem. If you work on a PC but the publisher uses Macs, for example, your copy in Word should be readable in Word for Mac. You don't use Word? No problem! Almost any word processor can save your manuscript in almost any other word processor format. If all else fails, save your manuscript as a "Rich Text" file; that will make it readable to any computer.

Sample 1 is a passage from my novel *Greenmagic*. (I blush to admit that the original manuscript was in a sans serif font. We learn something every day.)

MANUSCRIPT PAGE

(14-point Times New Roman)

Chapter 1

The squadron had been training all day in the fields south of the river, charging and wheeling and charging again until the horses were lathered and even Demazakh the training officer was tired and sweaty. The early spring sun was warm, even as it sank toward the distant mountains.

"Form up by twos," Demazakh rasped. The squadron obeyed, leaving only Dheribi alone at the rear of the column. He sat erect in his saddle, ignoring the dust in his eyes and the stink of horse dung and unwashed men. Tonight was Seventh Night, the eve of a day of freedom. Tonight he could bathe in peace, sleep in a clean bed, and wake to spend First Day with his books and focusing exercises. Tomorrow night he would be back in barracks for another week, but tomorrow night was still a long time off.

15

Selling Your Story

Writing the novel is the easy part. Now you've got to take the manuscript into a very tough marketplace. Publishers buy manuscripts that they think will make money — or at least attract enough readers to make the author's second or third book profitable. By definition, an author with a good sales record has an advantage over an unknown, unpublished writer. Even the unknowns have survived a Darwinian selection process just to get that manuscript completed. So here's some advice on how to stay in the process and see your book in print.

THE QUERY LETTER

The query letter can be a quick way for you to find out whether your novel might be of interest to a particular publisher — without having to wait until some editor finds your manuscript deep within her slush pile.

The query should give the editor an idea of your story (and a sense of the way you're handling it) that's clear enough to help her decide if it's worth considering. If the idea sounds good, you know the complete manuscript (or sample chapters) will enjoy a prompt and careful reading. If the idea doesn't sound right for that publishing house, the editor may tell you why, and perhaps suggest either a new approach or another publisher. (Either way, it's invaluable advice from an expert.)

Query Letter Guidelines

Some query letters are very short, and others are long indeed — novel outlines masquerading as letters. Consider the following suggestions as guidelines, not ironclad laws:

(a) Supply a short, lively description of what the book is about: A desperate attempt to escape a sorcerer's revenge, an unexpected journey that leads to romance and danger in 2025 China, an aging soldier's attempt to prove himself again in the Mexican Revolution of 2013.

(b) If not obvious from your plot summary, identify the audience your book is aimed at: hard-core space-opera fans, teenage girls, urban fantasy readers.

(c) Tell the editor what makes this novel different from others in the genre: a twist in the plot, a new angle on the hero, an unusual setting.

(d) Tell the editor your credentials. They may be helpful, if only as a dedicated and knowledgeable reader in the genre, or as an observant resident of the city you've set your novel in. These are not trivial qualifications: if you don't know and love the genre you're writing in, it will show. And if you don't know the history and folklore of your setting, the story will lack depth.

(e) Display in your query some of the excitement and energy you want to bring to your story — show how and why this story matters to you, and it'll matter to your editor.

Ideally, your query letter ought to run to a page or a little more, organized something like this:

First paragraph: Tell the editor what kind of novel you've written or are now writing. How long is it, when and where is it set? Describe the hero and perhaps one or two other major characters. What's their predicament? How are they proposing to get out of it? And why should readers care — that is, what's at stake?

Second paragraph: Describe what happens in the middle of the novel — how your characters interact, what conflicts arise among them.

Third paragraph: Describe the resolution of the novel — the climax and its outcome, and tying up of loose ends.

Fourth paragraph: Tell the editor why this story interests you, what your qualifications are for writing it, what other projects you're working on. The publisher's website will probably have told you the details of submitting your manuscript. If not, ask if they'd like the whole thing, or a sample plus outline.

Obviously this pattern will vary depending on the nature of your query. If it's just a letter, the plot summary will need to be fairly extensive. If you've included a stand-alone synopsis (see below) and some sample chapters, the cover query letter won't have to supply much of a plot summary at all. The letter in that case will focus on your background, your excitement about the story, and your questions for the editor.

Both writers and editors often use the terms *synopsis, summary,* and *outline* interchangeably, but for our purposes I'll define them more distinctly:

(a) *Synopsis:* Accompanies a sample of your manuscript. It describes the events of the story from beginning to end (or picks up from the end of your sample chapters). The synopsis may break your story down chapter by chapter or may simply relate events in a series of paragraphs. A synopsis usually begins with a title and byline; it may also include some introductory background information about the world of your story.

(b) *Summary:* The gist of your story, forming part of a query letter. My letter to the publisher Lester del Rey, pitching *Greenmagic,* included a summary.

(c) *Outline:* Your plan for the story, which may or may not look much like the synopsis or summary to send to your editor.

So you have several choices when approaching a publisher:

(a) Query letter alone, including a fairly detailed plot summary

(b) Query letter with plot summary, plus sample chapters

(c) Query letter with no plot summary, but with synopsis and chapters

Don't assume that a synopsis without chapters will sell your novel. The editor will want to see how you actually bring your story to life.

The query letter is a blurb for your novel, and like any blurb it needs to pique readers' interest and make them wonder: "How is *that* going to turn out?" The quality of writing in the query had better be first-rate, especially if you haven't included an elegantly written chapter or two. If your query is clumsy or riddled with errors, the editor will be less than eager to see more of your prose.

Because the query requires little time to read and respond to, it can help you quickly identify potential markets and definite non-markets. But it can't pre-sell your novel; at best, it can create only a cautiously welcoming attitude in an editor.

WILL THEY STEAL YOUR IDEA?

Will your query reveal such a knockout story idea that the publisher will steal it — turn you down, pass on your idea to one of the company's hack writers, and publish it for its own profit? This may be the single most common anxiety of novices, but the sad truth is that your idea probably isn't worth stealing. In fact, the editor may wearily see it as the umpteenth variation on some ancient plot, one she has seen a dozen times just this week.

This is not to say your idea should be positively weird; most story ideas in genre fiction really are variations on ancient plots. The trick is to make the variations appear to be fresh, surprising, and full of potential storytelling power.

Sample 2 is a copy of the letter I wrote proposing *Greenmagic* to the publisher Lester del Rey. It took the form of a query letter with a detailed plot summary. I could rely on the publisher's familiarity with my science fiction novels, but even a professional in a new genre can be just another novice — especially when the editor himself has been a highly successful professional longer than the author has been alive! (I should also point out that the eventual novel departed in many ways from the outline given here. As long as your departures work, the editor shouldn't mind.)

As it turned out, I couldn't finish *Greenmagic* until the spring of 1990, which was too late for prompt publication. So it had to wait until the spring of 1992, four years after I first proposed it. The moral of the story is that you should never promise a complete manuscript for an earlier date than you can realistically manage.

THE STORY SYNOPSIS

The story synopsis can take many forms; it has no rigid format. But the synopsis, like the manuscript, should be double-spaced and highly legible, with frequent paragraphing.

Some synopses cover the whole story while others supplement a portion of completed manuscript and presuppose the reader's familiarity with that portion. If you have broken your novel into chapters, you can divide your synopsis the same way. You may find, however, that what you thought would fit into one chapter will expand into two or three.

The major element of the synopsis, and sometimes the only element, is the narrative. Sample 3 shows the main features of a typical story synopsis.

A list of major characters' names (with brief descriptions) can sometimes be helpful in keeping the story straight; if used, such a list usually goes at the beginning of the synopsis.

A background section sometimes precedes the synopsis itself, especially if the story's context requires some explanation. This seems especially true of science fiction and fantasy, where the plot may hinge on unfamiliar story elements (like "wetware" and "jack joints"). Otherwise, such explanation simply crops up where required in the synopsis.

How long should a synopsis be? I've sold some novels with just two or three pages. Other writers may write 40 or 50 pages of outline. If your purpose is to interest an editor before the novel is completed, and you expect the total manuscript to run to 90,000 to 120,000 words, a synopsis of four to ten double-spaced pages should be adequate. After all, you're trying to tempt the editor by showing a brief sample, giving her grounds for a decision without a long investment in reading time.

Should you stick to your synopsis when you write your story? Not necessarily. It's there to help you and your editor, not to dictate the whole story. Like the itinerary of a foreign tour, it should give you a sense of direction and purpose while leaving you free to explore interesting byways; it should also give you a quick return to the main road if the byway turns into a dead end.

The query in Sample 2 was a direct approach to an editor. But you may well be aware that many, many publishing houses no longer even consider queries or submissions that do not come through an agent. Let's consider what that implies in the selling of your novel in the next chapter.

SAMPLE 2
QUERY LETTER WITH PLOT SUMMARY

March 21, 1988

Dear Mr. del Rey,

Owen Lock recently suggested that I consider doing a fantasy novel, and followed up by sending me a number of recent Del Rey fantasy titles. The idea interested me from the start. After nine SF novels a change of genre sounded like fun, and I've always enjoyed fantasy.

So I've been reading some of the books Owen sent, and thinking about fantasy in general and Del Rey's requirements in particular. Here's the germ of an idea you might find worth considering.

One of the conventions of the form seems to be that political power must be gained and kept through magic, but that magicians rarely exercise power directly. This has always seemed a little strange to me — like Lee Iacocca acting as a "consultant" to some nebbish who happens to be a descendant of the original Chrysler. In Tolkien I can accept that Gandalf's job is indeed that of an advisor: we have an organization here in Canada that ships retired executives overseas to supply administrative wisdom to Third World companies, and Gandalf is doing something very similar in Middle Earth.

Some writers — including your own Barbara Hambly — suggest that the practice of magic is so fascinating and obsessive that magicians have no interest in the tedium of running a kingdom. When they do seek political power, their efforts are destructive and have to be undone by a hero who may be helped by some other magician.

The message in fantasy is always a pretty conservative one: We have come to a pretty pass, and drastic action is needed to put matters back as they once were in some ideal past. That ideal past is usually some form of feudalism; its modern forms don't look very pretty in Latin America, and it probably wasn't all that satisfying in medieval Europe.

The medieval European feudalists, however, had terrific media relations (apart from guys like Cervantes) — so good that people still get a bang out of knight-errantry, dragonslaying and sorcery.

Well, I'm thinking about a story in which the knights are low-tech Hell's Angels, their tame magicians are amoral neurotics, and there are no good old days to restore. If Earthsea's mages had to maintain a Balance, in my world it's a balance of terror: no magician gets a chance to become too powerful, because his jealous colleagues will gang up to destroy him. It's a world of black magic serving political causes, white magic serving personal desires — and green magic to combat oppression.

My story is called *Greenmagic*. It takes place in a world much like ours, but in which human tribes contend for a place with other races and beings. Magic works here, and it does indeed lock its practitioners into a trance-like state. To gain resources magicians work for warlords, who battle endlessly with one another and use magic as a convenient supplement to swords and catapults.

Some centuries before the story begins, the warlords' ancestors swept into a broad land of plains and mountains, conquering the simple farming tribes who had inhabited the land for millennia. Broken and enslaved, the natives are now a class of serfs. They support the warlords, as well as magicians, artisans, and merchants, in a mosaic of city-states.

Some of the serfs have escaped into the mountains, where they live precariously: the warlords' sons make forays into the mountaineer villages as a form of combat training. They also take slaves from the mountaineers, usually women.

One such mountaineer slave woman is pregnant. She bears her son on the manor of a warlord, names him Mory, and rears him in her traditions — including mountaineer magic, which he has a talent for. As he grows older, Mory's abilities attract the attention of a magician who takes him as an apprentice. The magician serves an ambitious warlord who dreams of building an empire, but foreign magicians use an unusual spell that drives Mory's master into a state of "lucid insanity": he sees the futility and misery of magic-supported warrior states, and refuses to follow his warlord's commands.

The warlord executes his magician, and nearly does the same to Mory. But the young apprentice escapes, taking with him his master's lorebooks and apparatus — including the staff of Askeron, a powerful weapon in both physical and magical conflict, which other magicians would very much like to possess.

Hunted by his warlord and by enemy magicians, Mory escapes with the help of a serf girl and the Burrowers — ancient relatives of the serfs who have hidden from the warlords in vast networks of caves and tunnels. Some of his old master's lucid insanity has invaded Mory's mind; he begins to dream of overthrowing the whole warlord society.

To do so, however, he must learn a great deal more magic, and to risk death not only from the warlords and magicians, but from the supernatural forces they are tampering with. In the process he gains an understanding of what he begins to call "greenmagic," a force that adds to the order and harmony in the world rather than lessening them.

By the end of the tale, Mory has gathered a force of human and inhuman allies against the warlords. In a climactic battle, greenmagic faces its harshest test and Mory is tempted to abandon it for the black magic of his enemies. In the end greenmagic triumphs and the warlords yield to Mory. His allies want to make him emperor, but he refuses: they must build their own society and run it themselves.

Obviously the success of a story like this will depend upon the vividness and believability of the fantasy world, and upon the characters and incidents. My almost-fantasy, *Eyas*, ought to give you some idea of how well I can do in this field. If you think the idea merits a more detailed outline, I'd be glad to develop one for you. Presumably the story would run about 100,000 words. My current novel, *Gryphon*, should be finished about the end of this summer, and if we made *Greenmagic* the next project it could be in your hands by the summer of '89. I look forward to your response.

FEATURES OF A STORY SYNOPSIS

Bloodware
A novel by Jo Doakes
1234 Downs Street
North Vancouver, BC V7G 1H7
Canada
jdoakes@intergate.bc.ca
Tel: (604) 989-6677

Background
In the mid-21st century, a huge illegal industry has
sprung up to create and distribute "wetware" —
organic computer circuitry that can create
addictively powerful hallucinations. Once implanted
with the right circuits, users can induce the
hallucinations by logging in to "jack joints." These
are illegal servers operating deep in the Labyrinth,
the highly developed Internet of the 2020s.
"Ariadnes" (specialists in Labyrinth navigation) are
too few to track all the jack joints, and police are
therefore helpless against spreading plague.

Characters
Jenny Chan, 22, a young Ariadne looking for
    adventure
Donald Matthews, 24, a wetware developer
Kenneth Holwood, 44, Matthew's business partner

*You don't need to list
every character, just
the key people in the
story.*

Chapter One
On a fine spring day in 2023, Jenny Chan applies for
a job working for a mysterious millionaire. The
interview goes well. Her new boss is Donald
Matthews, a handsome businessman scarcely older
than Jenny, but with an unsavory reputation as a
designer of illegal wetware.

*A few more lines of
summary should cover
the chapter. Note that
no dialogue is used;
simply summarize
what is said or the
outcome of a
conversation.*

Chapter Two

Hurrying home after escaping the police raid, Jenny bumps into Kenneth Holwood, Donald's former partner. Holwood seems deranged, and hints at some terrible secret in Donald's past. The next morning Jenny mails the encrypted file despite her qualms; she wonders what it might contain. Meanwhile, in a shabby hotel room across town, Holwood meticulously plans the death of Donald Matthews.

This shows that the story's point of view is third person omniscient and that the point of view may change as events require.

16

Researching Publishers and Agents

Too many people submit manuscripts to publishers. Simply to read enough of those manuscripts to judge them unworthy would take the full-time services of several salaried editors. Most publishers simply can't afford to plow through the slush pile in hopes of some-day finding a Great Novelist.

So they indicate on their websites and in *Writer's Market* that they will consider only agented submissions — work that a profes-sional literary agent, who knows the market, thinks has some sales potential.

That simply draws fire onto the agents, who now find that they too have huge slush piles. And, like the publishers, the agents can't make money reading junk. Where does that leave you?

In better shape than you think. If you've hammered out a cred-ible but surprising plot about interesting people in a hell of a jam, and you're showing them in action instead of telling us what they're

like, and your grammar, spelling, and punctuation are first-rate —
you're already ahead of 80 percent of your competition.

FINDING THE RIGHT PUBLISHER

Too many novice writers simply fire off their work to a publisher
they've vaguely heard of, or one that's supposed to be prestigious,
or even one that happens to be conveniently located right in town.
(Those were precisely my three motives in submitting my first children's book to Parnassus Press. They bought it, which shows that
sometimes even ignoramuses can get lucky. By rights I should have
had to send the manuscript to a couple of dozen houses before hit-
ting the right one — or not.)

Target Markets

Publishers tend to carve out special markets for themselves. A
couple of sharp editors can dominate a genre; because they know
how to reach a certain kind of reader, they attract a certain kind of
writer. Or a publisher may be passionately devoted to supporting a
certain kind of fiction but is deeply uninterested in any other kind.
A feminist publisher wouldn't have the faintest idea how to market
a men's action-adventure novel, and wouldn't care to learn. A children's publisher won't care how well crafted your murder mystery
is. And so on.

So step one is almost embarrassingly obvious: Notice which
houses publish the kind of story you're working on. Look carefully
at the story elements in the titles they publish; Del Rey fantasy novels, for example, require magic as a major component, not just as
frosting or a gimmick to get the hero somewhere interesting. Out
of all the publishers in North America, only a few are potentially
yours.

Resources

Then consult those potential publishers' websites and entries in
Writer's Market and see what they have to say about their own needs
and who their editors are in specific genres. You may learn that your

work in progress is too long, or too short, or needs some particular quality like a hero aged over 35 years. You may also learn how long it takes them to respond to queries and submissions. Don't take those statements as legally binding promises; responses almost always take far longer, especially for unagented submissions.

Writer's Market also lists publishers by the genres they publish. This list can lead you to publishing houses you're not familiar with, but don't just rush off your manuscript. Check out the entries of these houses, and also track down some of their recent titles in your genre. If they strike you as dreadful garbage, avoid them. Better to stay unpublished than to be trapped with a bad publisher.

Another useful source of information is the publishing trade press. The magazines *Publisher's Weekly* in the United States and *Quill and Quire* in Canada are much more up to date than any annual can be. So if the top military science fiction editor in New York has just moved to a new publisher, or a publisher is starting a new line of fantasy novels aimed at young adults, you may adjust your marketing strategy accordingly. Magazines like *The Writer* and *Writer's Digest* supply similar market news.

FINDING AN AGENT

If every possible publisher warns you off with "No unagented submissions," you then have to go through a similar process with literary agents. You should be able to find an annually updated list of agents in your local library or the reference section of a good bookstore. Some agents, like Richard Curtis and the late Scott Meredith, have even written books themselves about the publishing business; these are worth reading.

Which Type of Agent Is Right for You?

As a general rule, you probably need an agent in the city where most of your publishers are. That, as a general rule, means New York City. You also need an agent who knows the market for your particular genre, so your work will go as promptly as possible to the most likely markets. (Some agents may submit a work in multiple copies to all potential publishers; this can really speed up the process.)

But also bear in mind that phone, fax, and email can put almost anyone in close touch with the New York market, so an agent in Chicago or Los Angeles or Miami may be quite as effective as somebody in Manhattan — and may also be familiar with regional publishers.

Consider whether you want a big agent with scores or hundreds of clients, or a small outfit. The big agent may have clout but little stake in promoting you; the small agent may work hard for you, but lack entrée to some editors. Talk to published writers, if possible, about their experiences with agents. Sometimes a sympathetic author can suggest a good one, but don't expect an automatic warm welcome from the agent just because you dropped a name. You still have to rely on your own merits.

No agent, however good, can sell your work to an editor who doesn't want to buy it. What the agent offers the editor is a reasonably trustworthy opinion about the marketability of a particular manuscript. It's in the agent's interest to deal only in work with serious sales potential, and to get it quickly into the hands of its most likely buyers.

You may therefore have to query a number of agents before you find one who's willing to take you on. And you may find that some agents won't look at your stuff unless you pay them to.

This is a highly controversial practice, and many writers and agents really resent it. You will get a quick response, however. The agent will read your manuscript and offer you feedback. Sometimes you'll get a detailed critique that may devastate your ego but teach you just what you need to learn. On the other hand, you may get nothing useful at all. Unless you're really desperate, I suggest you avoid fee-charging agents.

Sometimes an agent will take you on but strongly suggest certain kinds of revisions, or even that you tackle a completely different kind of story. Listen carefully; you're getting advice from someone who knows the market and wants to share in your prosperity. At least one of my novels greatly profited from the advice of an agent who thought my proposed ending was a disaster.

The Agent's Contract

Your agreement with an agent may take the form of a detailed contract, or a simple agreement over the phone, or something in between. Be sure you understand and accept the terms your agent requires: 10 percent of what he or she makes you, or 15 percent? Deductions for photocopying, postage, and phone bills? Control over all your writing, or just your fiction output?

Once you have an agent, don't be a pest. When your agent has got something to report, he or she will let you know. If you've got something to report, like the completion of the manuscript or an idea for turning it into a series, let the agent know. Otherwise, stay off the phone and stick to your writing.

What If I've Already Found a Publisher?

In some cases, of course, you may find you've sold a novel on your own hook and then decide to go looking for an agent. Under these happy circumstances you should find it fairly easy to get an agent's interest. If the publisher's already offered you a contract (and you haven't signed yet), the agent may be willing to take you on and then bargain a better deal for you.

But you'll probably do all right even if you negotiate that first contract on your own. Most publishers are honorable and decent people; sometimes their integrity is positively intimidating. Even if they weren't honorable, your first book is likely to make so little money that it wouldn't be worth it to rob you. The next chapter discusses the publishing contract in more detail.

17

The Publishing Contract

When you do finally receive a publisher's contract, you may feel your heart sink. It will likely run to several pages of single-spaced text, highly flavored with legalese and organized in a daunting sequence of numbered paragraphs and subparagraphs. Who knows what thorns lurk in such a thicket?

Actually, not too many. Most of your contract is boilerplate, standard text that protects you as much as it does the publisher. It is often possible, even for a novice, to negotiate specific aspects of the contract.

Still, it helps to know what you're getting yourself into, so let us take a look at some of the key passages you're likely to find in your contract.

DELIVERY OF SATISFACTORY COPY

If you're selling your novel on the strength of sample chapters and an outline, the publisher wants assurance that you'll submit the full manuscript (often both hard copy and an electronic version), at an agreed-upon length, by an agreed-upon date. If your full manuscript doesn't measure up, or arrives too late, the publisher has the contractual right to demand return of any money you've received.

In practice, the publisher is usually much more flexible. He or she may bounce your manuscript back to you with a reminder that you don't get the rest of your advance until the manuscript is "satisfactory." The publisher (or more likely the editor) will tell you in exquisite detail what you still need to do to achieve "satisfactory" status.

A late manuscript also means you won't collect the balance of your advance until it arrives, and it may also cause delays in final publication, as I learned to my sorrow with *Greenmagic.* In extreme cases, the publisher may cancel publication and demand a return of any advance already paid to you.

PERMISSION FOR USE OF COPYRIGHTED MATERIAL

If you want to include the lyrics of a pop song in your novel, or quote something as an epigraph, it's up to you to obtain permission from the copyright holder to reproduce his or her material in your novel, and to pay to do so, if necessary. Ask your publisher or editor for guidelines in obtaining permissions, including which rights to ask for — U.S., North American, world? for all editions or this edition only? for all languages or just the English language? etc.

If you leave it to the publisher, he will charge you; if the publisher can't get permission and the novel doesn't work without such material, the deal is off and you have to repay any advance you've received. Obviously, this is an extreme case; normally you just drop the lines from the song or poem, and carry on.

Copyright scares a lot of apprentice writers. It's beginning to scare a lot of other people as well, especially with the explosive growth of the World Wide Web and the rest of the Internet. So much material is appearing online that copyright violations are becoming routine (especially with the copying of news stories). Many countries are revising their copyright laws, compounding confusion at least until the laws are passed and interpreted by the courts. It's somewhat less of a problem with fiction, but you should make yourself familiar with your country's basic laws on intellectual property in general and copyright in particular.

GRANT OF RIGHTS

In the clause concerning the grant of rights, you are giving the publisher the right to make copies of what you've written. These copies may be in hardcover, softcover, audio cassette, filmstrip, comic book, or whatever. You are also specifying in which parts of the world the publisher may sell such copies. For example, a sale to a British publisher may specifically exclude North America, leaving you free to sell North American rights separately.

You may also be giving the publisher rights to sell foreign translations, to print excerpts in other books or periodicals as a form of advertising, or to sell copies to book clubs. Normally such sales require your informed, written consent.

Your contract may specify that rights remain with the original publisher as long as any editions (including foreign translations) are in print. If the contract you asked to sign has this clause, you may want to negotiate something better. Otherwise your book may be unavailable for republishing in English just because it's still in print in Argentina or Israel.

PROOFREADING AND AUTHOR'S CORRECTIONS

You agree that you will proofread the galleys or page proofs of your novel and return the corrected pages promptly. If your changes amount to actual revision of the original manuscript and will require retypesetting more than 10 percent of the book, the publisher will charge you for such costs. This can very easily destroy any income you might have earned from the book.

ADVANCES AND ROYALTIES

The advance and royalty clause spells out how much the publisher will pay you, and when.

Advances

The most common agreement is payment of one-third of the advance on signing the contract; one-third on delivery of a satisfactory complete manuscript; and one-third on publication date. You may be able to negotiate half on signing and half on delivery; otherwise, you are in effect lending the publisher some of your advance until a publication date that may be over a year away.

Royalties

Royalties are generally a percentage of the list price of the book. For hardcover books, the usual royalty is 10 percent of list price. So a novel retailing for $24.95 will earn its author $2.50 per copy. For mass-market paperbacks, royalty rates can range from 4 percent to 8 percent, usually with a proviso that the rate will go up after a huge number of copies sell — 150,000 seems to be a popular target. A paperback selling at $7.95, with an 8 percent royalty, will therefore earn you about 64¢. A trade paperback will probably earn a comparable rate; the list price, however, will likely be higher and the number of copies sold will be lower.

Whatever the royalty rates, you're likely to get only half as much for sales to book clubs or overseas markets. This is especially painful for Canadian authors with American publishers: sales in your own country, as "foreign" sales, earn only half the U.S. royalty rate. (For more information, see the essay on royalties on this book's CD.)

Licensing Sales

You will also agree to split the take from certain kinds of licensing sales. For example, if your novel is a hardcover and some other house wants to bring out a paperback edition, you can usually expect a 50 percent share of what the paperback house pays. Sometimes a paperback house will license a hardcover edition (in hopes of getting more critical attention for your book — as hardcover books do — and hence selling more copies in paperback eventually); in such a case you should expect 75 percent of the deal.

If you can possibly avoid it, do not agree to give your publisher a share of any sale to movies or television. A film or television show based on your novel will boost the publisher's sales quite nicely; he doesn't need a slice off the top of a deal that will surely pay you more than the publisher did. But if the book seems highly unlikely to interest Hollywood, you might offer a slice of film rights in exchange for a richer advance, with a proviso that an actual film or television sale will also produce an additional chunk of money from the publisher.

The publisher will usually not charge for the production of versions of your novel in braille or other formats for people with disabilities. So you will get no money from this source.

Royalty Statements

The publisher should agree to supply you with two royalty statements a year. Each will cover a six-month reporting period, and each should arrive about 90 days after the close of that period. So a statement for January to June should reach you at the end of September. This will probably be a computer printout, and may be a bit confusing. But you should be able to make out the number of copies shipped, the number returned unsold by booksellers (known as *returns*), and the number presumably sold. The publisher will hold back on some of the royalty against further returns. Whatever remains is the actual number on which the publisher owes you money.

Chances are that your advance will have consumed any potential royalties for the first reporting period, and perhaps for the second as well. Once you have earned out your advance, however, you should expect a check with each royalty statement.

Your contract should explicitly promise you at least two royalty statements a year. No promise? No deal. Some publishers promise a statement only after the novel has earned out its advance. This means you may go for years — or forever — without knowing what your sales have been.

AUTHOR'S WARRANTIES AND INDEMNITIES

In the warranty and indemnity clause, you are promising that the manuscript you are submitting is indeed your work, that it isn't obscene, a breach of privacy, libelous, or otherwise illegal.

If you do get into legal trouble about what you've said in your novel, you agree to cooperate with the publisher's legal defense, and you agree to pay your share of the costs instead of asking the publisher, booksellers, or others to do so. If the publisher's lawyer thinks the manuscript poses legal problems, you agree to make the changes required to solve those problems — or to allow the publisher to do so.

You may find an insurance rider as part of your contract; this is intended to protect both you and the publisher from suffering total financial disaster if you get caught in a losing lawsuit.

AUTHOR'S COPIES

You will get a certain number of free copies of your printed book and will pay a reduced rate for more copies. That means you will still pay for those copies, as you should.

OPTION CLAUSE

Pay attention to the option clause! This clause says you are giving the publisher right of first refusal on your next book (or at least your next book in this particular genre). The option clause means the publisher will give the next book a close, prompt reading. You should expect a response within 90 days, but some contracts specify 90 days after publication of your current book. That means you might have to wait for months, maybe over a year, until the publisher sees the initial reaction to your first book.

In practice, though, you probably will get a quicker response than that. If the publisher does make you an offer, you have the right to refuse it; you can then take your second book to any other publisher you like. However, you can't sell it to anyone else unless you get better terms for it than your original publisher offered.

You may well find yourself trapped as a result. If you need the money in a hurry, you may feel you've got to accept a bad offer rather than spend months or years shopping your manuscript around the market until you find a more generous publisher. And then, of course, your second contract will include an option clause for the third novel.

Your best hope in this case is that sales of the first book will warrant a heftier advance on the second or third book. And if the publisher still won't cooperate, you can then go to another publisher with at least some respectable sales figures that show you deserve a better deal.

GOING OUT OF PRINT

If the publisher lets your novel go out of print, you can make a formal request for it to be reprinted; if the publisher doesn't want to reprint it, you can then demand that all rights revert to you. You are then free to sell the book to another publisher. I have done this a couple of times. You don't make as much money on the resale, but at least the book stays out on the market longer.

You will probably not make any money from *remaindered* copies that the publisher may sell to a book jobber at a deep discount. Some contracts, however, may pay the author a percentage of such sales. It's also possible to buy copies of your book at a similar low price.

A WORD OF ADVICE

If at all possible, go over the contract with the editor or publisher, asking whatever questions arise. Then take your contract to an agent, lawyer, or professional writer. Chances are that the contract is perfectly okay. But even if you don't find something sneaky in the fine print, you'll have a clearer understanding of what you and your publisher have committed yourselves to. If something arises later on, like a problem over the option clause or the frequency of royalty statements, it won't come as a total shock.

Conclusion

IS IT WORTH DOING AT ALL?

You might think, if you've come this far, that writing science fiction and fantasy (and any other kind of literature) is strictly for lucky geniuses and lunatics. Hardly anyone has really original ideas, even fewer people put them down on paper, fewer still manage to finish them or send them off to a publisher, and only a tiny minority seem to get published. Of these, only a still smaller minority actually make more than a few thousand dollars out of endless toil. You may recall that Dr. Samuel Johnson observed over 200 years ago: "No man but a blockhead ever wrote, except for money."

Well, I beg to differ. The real blockheads in this business are those who write only for money. I've been a blockhead myself a couple of times, accepting projects because they brought big advances or because I thought I needed the money. Completing those novels was not only painful but boring, because I didn't have some inner drive to write them — only the dangled carrot of a check when the project was done.

Making money from your writing is great, but you should treat it as a windfall — like finding a $20 bill when you're walking the dog. Tomorrow you'll walk the dog again, and you'll both be the better for it. But don't feel like a failed dog walker if you find no money next time.

When you think about it, we work so we can make money so we can afford to do things that don't make money: watch movies, read books, go skiing, walk the dog ... and write fiction.

These kinds of activities are their own reward, and in the case of writing fiction, the rewards are considerable.

First of all, it's great entertainment to master any craft. Once, while visiting the studio of a professional basket weaver, I realized that weaving baskets might be mental therapy, but it is also a highly complex skill; it requires powers of spatial visualization that I, for one, totally lack. If I could gain those powers by systematic, persistent practice, I would eventually rewire my brain to think as the professional basket weaver did. And then not only would I become different, but the world I perceived would become different too. Even if the practice was frustrating and maddening, it would be immense fun to make any progress at all.

So if you can't bend willow withes into a usable and beautiful basket, maybe you can link words together into some kind of usable and beautiful story. In the process you may become frustrated and maddened, but you'll also see that you can make at least some progress. The more you persist, the more you rewire your brain to think like a writer.

After a while it becomes a self-sustaining process: words and images echo in your mind, generating more words and images. Everything you read helps to keep the process going. If it's junk, you see why it's junk. If it's brilliant, you probably can't see how the author did it, so you read it more closely and critically. Whether consciously or not, you absorb the language and cadences of the writers you admire.

Eventually, as I've suggested earlier in this book, you find yourself in a kind of long conversation with every author you've ever read. You're responding to them on their own terms; your story, however humbly, answers theirs.

My own books are my side of a 50-year conversation I've been having with Robert Heinlein, Alfred Bester, Jack Vance, L. Sprague de Camp, Ursula K. Le Guin, and many others. They all paid me the compliment of thinking I was worth telling stories to; I have tried to return the compliment, and to pass it along. If the authors that matter to you have inspired similar feelings, then you have another good reason for writing.

Writing science fiction and fantasy is also a superb form of self-education. You really learn when you research a story or novel. You don't know when you'll stumble over some amazing fact or speculation that will make your vague idea suddenly crystallize into a real story — or when you'll wander into a wine store and find Juvenal himself ready to guide you through Rome's night streets. Maybe you didn't think ancient history, or grammar, or college chemistry was all that fascinating when you had to study it. But now you really have to study it — and it's more fun than you ever imagined. Why? Because now you're learning for yourself and your readers, not just for a diploma or degree.

Writing is a solitary task, and plenty of writers complain about how lonely it is. But plenty of others find a real comradeship with other writers, apprentice or professional. Like any complex craft, it offers endless opportunities for shoptalk — both the actual story-telling and talking about the nuts and bolts of telling stories. The aspiring writer can bask in the mentor's attention, or battle the rival's criticism, and grow stronger from both. After all, we need to know both our talents and our weaknesses.

Even if you're a true solitary, a kind of companionship comes from the characters you create. Live with them for a year or two of writing, and they'll never leave you.

This is also a craft that you never finish learning. If language itself is fractal, infinitely complex at every level, then writing poses challenges for the professional as well as the apprentice. The only way writing can become boring is by the writer's refusal to pay attention to it. Every manuscript is trying to tell its author something new about writing and about the author, but not every author listens.

You can never become complacent or think you know everything about the craft. As soon as you do, some reader or fellow writer will drop a casual remark that makes you feel totally ignorant. Don't feel dismayed — after all, it means you have more to learn about writing, about yourself, and about the human condition.

George Orwell once observed that, from the inside, every life feels like a failure. Spoken like a true writer! If you publish your story in a webzine, you feel like a failure because you didn't get paid and hardly anyone read your work. If you publish with a big New York house and your book sells 100,000 copies, you feel like a failure because you didn't get a big enough advance and hardly anyone read it — compared to Stephen King or Diana Gabaldon.

But that sense of failure, I suggest, is a deception. To conceive, write, revise, and publish any story are real achievements. When you achieve any of these things, you have achieved something special.

Is it worth doing? Yes.

Appendix:
An Annotated
Work in Progress

Below is the first chapter of a novel I'm working on called *Henderson's Tenants*. I've interrupted the narrative with comments on some of the key points I'm trying to establish in the chapter — points that I will expand on in later chapters.

CHAPTER 1

Friday, June 14

"No way to break the news gently, Mike." Jeremy Stein came around his desk and sank into the armchair next to Mike Henderson's. Awkwardly, he patted Mike's shoulder. "You've got advanced pancreatic cancer."

Mike looked into Jer's eyes. But Jer seemed to be at the end of a long tunnel, very far away. Mike felt far away from himself. Familiar stress response.

"That's what I suspected," he heard himself saying. "The symptoms were getting pretty obvious." And even more obvious when Jer had asked for a face-to-face to talk about the diagnosis.

[We start by putting the hero under serious stress. We also establish the point of view: Third person limited, inside Mike's head. He knows himself well enough to understand why he's reacting as he is. He "hears himself" as if someone else were doing the talking — and the story will show he has multiple selves.]

"It's stage three, T3, which means it's spread to your stomach and colon as well as your pancreas. I'm really pissed off that you didn't see me way before this. You're as bad as a doctor about ignoring your health."

"Worse. But I've been a little busy lately."

Jer shook his head and rolled his eyes. "Hey. How long have we known each other? First year at McGill?"

"Yeah. September '95. Thirty-five years almost."

[We establish the relationship between Mike and Jer — old friends who can speak bluntly to each other — and set the time: 2030. Canadian readers will recognize McGill as a good university in Montreal. We will soon establish the setting as Canada — mostly in the suburb of North Vancouver, BC.]

"And you were always an asshole about your health. You smoked for what, ten, fifteen years? Thought you'd live forever."

"Twelve years, actually."

"What I said, you're an asshole. An unlucky asshole, because usually people get this when they're sixty-five, seventy. You're way ahead of the pack."

"Okay, what can I do about it?"

Jer shrugged. "We can try a couple of therapies, mostly chemo, but pancreatic cancer is still a bastard. Even stem cells—"

"So I've got about seven months."

"Done your homework! Actually, that's just an average from the time of diagnosis, so you could last a lot longer."

Mike drew a long breath. "Or a lot less. Well, I'd rather hear it from a friend than some flunky in an HMO."

[We're learning more about what's at stake for Mike; we also learn that American-style health management organizations are the alternative to this kind of personal care.]

"Hey, my pleasure." Jeremy reached out and patted Mike's shoulder again. "Mike, I am so sorry. You sure didn't deserve this."

"No one does."

"You should talk to Moira."

"Oh, I don't think so. She's busy with her new family. She wasn't interested in getting in touch during the trial."

"Still, you guys were married, what, fifteen years? Kind of tacky not to tell her."

"Yeah. I'll get around to it. First I want to get organized about this."

[This means Moira is going to show up later in the story; if she doesn't, I'll have to edit these lines out of the chapter. I still don't know what role she might play in the story.]

"Sure, of course. Let me give you the detailed diagnosis plus some diet suggestions. Your appetite's not going to improve, but you've still got to eat. Think about your options, then get back to me."

He handed Mike a stylus. Mike pressed it against his computer, taped to the skin just below the inside of his left elbow. It was an old one, a square black Macintosh 5 centimeters on a side and almost a centimeter thick. Jer's personal computer was a stylish blue disc tattooed on his left wrist, a Sungold no more than 3 centimeters across.

[We get a sense of how computers have evolved, with a hint
— about to be confirmed — that Mike can't afford as good
a computer as Jer can.]

Mike handed the stylus back. "I can't afford to see you until
next month."

Jeremy frowned. "You're not on Basic, are you?"

[We'll learn more about Basic Support soon.]

"No, but I've got a job that mostly pays the rent. And no health
plan."

"Aw, hell. Look, you come and see me next week. Professional
courtesy. After all you taught me about poker back in school, I owe
you."

"Well, that's very kind of you, Jer. Let me think about it."

"This is a goddamn scandal. One of the best scientists in Canada
— in the world. And you're broke? Jesus."

[We're gaining important background on Mike.]

Mike stood up. "I'm doing okay."

[Mike's calm responses are partly due to the stress of the
bad news, and partly just the way he is. When he fails to
repress his emotions, he'll real blow up.]

"You got screwed because Kosaki screwed up."

"I'm past all that. We were in the wrong field at the wrong
time."

"My ass. You were doing nanotech we really need. Not like that
sludge Kosaki was cranking out. Programmable bots, interactivity
— man, you were right there."

Mike smiled. "And now I'm right here. Doesn't matter."

"The hell it doesn't. Doing medicine isn't much fun anymore. I
was following what you were doing before they shut you down. Just
astounding stuff. Your bots would make life a lot easier."

Mike shrugged. "You know something, Jer? It was mostly spin. You get a few gimmicks like pixelite, and everyone thinks the Singularity is going to be next week. Then Kosaki has a problem, and it's really more like an epidemic than grey goo eating the world. So don't lose any sleep about it, eh?" He paused. "Let me think about what to do next. I'll get back to you next week, eh?"

[More exposition; we're learning why Mike doesn't have much money. Along with pixelite, we also mention the Singularity — the moment predicted by nanotech advocates when molecule-sized computers abruptly transform the world into one of unimaginably advanced technology and wealth. Once we've mentioned it, we'll have to deliver it, though in an unpredictable way.]

Jer sighed and nodded. "Your call. But if I don't hear from you by, what, next Tuesday, I'll call you."

"Good enough."

Jer handed him a small blue cardboard box. "This is a macho painkiller, Polyphonine, very new. Some people get fun side effects, almost hallucinogenic. But everybody gets pain relief. The research says, what, long-term use may lead to addiction. You should live so long."

["Polyphonine" means "many voices," like those heard by some people with mental illness. The drug is going to enable Mike to make critical breakthroughs in nanotech by putting him in closer contact with his nonconscious selves. He'll also learn that Jer has been set up to give him this drug as part of a scheme to exploit Mike's abilities.]

They shook hands, with Jer looking down at the floor. Mike walked out of the clinic waiting room, past two sad women waiting for their own bad news, into the empty Metrotown parking lot and across the lot to the SkyTrain station. Poor Jer: stuck in this dead mall, when all the successful doctors were in gated clinics in Point Grey or West Van. That's where youthful idealism would get you.

[Vancouverites will recognize the references; others will soon learn just where Mike is.]

He was aware of his new potbelly, incongruous on his lanky frame. His pants kept sagging down around his bony hips, reminding him of the weight he'd lost in the past month or two. That had been the tip-off, that and the perennial stomachache. He'd remembered enough from his year in med school to suspect what the problem was.

> [In third person limited POV, we see only what the character sees. All Mike notices about himself is the swelling of the tumor and the weight loss. We have no need for a more detailed description.]

He walked up the unpowered escalator to the platform. It was almost dark now; the North Shore mountains were dark against the sunset in the northwest. He remembered when they'd had skiing on Grouse and Seymour, back when Vancouver still got snow every winter. Now they just got rain — and in mid-June, not even that. The many fires of the last twenty years had scarred the dead forests on Grouse and Seymour into tiger stripes of black and orange. A poster flashed at him: *Save water today, enjoy it tomorrow!*

> [This paragraph is a casual reference to the impact of global warming: restricted energy, low rainfall, tree-killing pests.]

The trains didn't run very often these days, so the platform was crowded. He stood in the middle of the crowd on the westbound platform and scanned the others. Once he'd have seen only a blur of BSers, if he'd noticed them at all, but now that he was effectively one himself, he saw them in all their diversity.

Lots of geezers, late boomers who'd hit 65 after the pensions and jobs had dried up. They were the real BSers — without Basic Support, they'd die. Even more grannies, women in their seventies and eighties with slotted boxes welded to their walkers where people could drop coins that wouldn't be scooped out by the next person. Quite a few were immigrants, mostly Aussies these days, all wearing green lapel pins that tracked their travel and purchases. A couple of loony tunes, both of them shouting incoherently about whatever was troubling them. And lots of pogeys, the unemployed of all ages who lived on Basic Support plus whatever scams they could manage.

[Coming from a higher social class, Mike is a detached observer of the lower classes he now lives among. The reference to immigrants from Australia hints that life is not good Down Under.]

Mike guessed that he was a pogey and not a geezer. After all, he had a job, sort of. Fifty-three was too young for geezerhood.

Not too young to die, though.

[The diagnosis is beginning to sink in.]

"I'm possessed!" one of the loony tunes screamed. He was a man about Mike's age, with a scarred face and white stubble on his sagging cheeks. "Possessed by demons! Oh God, exorcise me! Drive them out of me into the Gadarene swine. Oh Jesus, save me from the demons!" A few people looked at him with mild interest; most ignored him.

[This is foreshadowing: Under the influence of the new drug, Mike is going to feel possessed as well by his various nonconscious selves.]

Mike pulled out his shades, one of the few expensive gadgets he'd managed to hold onto after the bankruptcy and the trial. They interacted beautifully with the Mac on his arm, much better than the cheap Chinese goggles most people settled for. When he tapped the earpiece, a ghostly interface appeared; he could still see the platform, but now a new figure stood among the BSers: a genii, swiped from a century-old movie called *The Thief of Baghdad*. He'd been using it for a couple of days, but could see it would soon get boring.

"What is your command, O master?"

"Review and summarize the files on pancreatic cancer. Then display the diagnosis and prognosis I just got from Jer Stein."

"Your wish is my command." The genii bowed and faded away.

[We see how Mike uses "shades," the computer interface of 2030; the genii is also a bit of foreshadowing, since Mike's nanobots will give him seemingly magical powers.]

One of the other people on the platform came alongside him and snatched the shades off his face. Mike tried to grab them back and felt a punch in his stomach. The pain was a lot more than he would have expected, and it felt natural to drop to all fours until the pain went away. That took a long time. He was dimly aware of the arrival of the train and the movement of people around him.

After a while the people were gone and so was the train. A couple of late arrivals came up to the platform but stayed well away from him.

Finally he pushed himself up off his knees and stepped back until he could sit down on the bench. His stomach still hurt a lot.

"Ah shit," he muttered. He looked around for a videocam. Maybe CanSec had actually seen who'd hit him, though no one had shown up to check. Finally he saw a couple of brackets up on a pillar where the cam had been ripped out. Typical.

[More stress for Mike — a kind of temporary blinding. We also see that no one comes to his aid; the Canada of 2030 has little social capital. CanSec is Canadian Security, a privatized version of the Royal Canadian Mounted Police.]

It was dark by the time the next train arrived and hauled him from Metrotown to the SeaBus terminal. The little ferry was crowded with more BSers. Amazing how you don't notice them for years, he thought. Why would you, when you're getting around in a company limo? Then you become one yourself, and they're everywhere. Especially on a Friday night in midmonth, when they've still got a little money to spend.

The trip across Burrard Inlet was oddly consoling. Vancouver was still a beautiful city, even if the downtown towers were mostly dark and empty and the docks hadn't seen a cruise ship in twenty years. A zeppelin was anchored on the North Shore side, lights gleaming along its sides under a huge, animated Chinese flag. It must be taking on lumber; the grain elevators, on the south side, were deserted as usual. Mike remembered driving across the Prairies back in '25: where the wheat and canola had once made great checkerboards of green and yellow, now everything was beige and tan, and you could buy a Saskatchewan town just by moving in and spending ten thousand dollars in improvements. But ten grand wouldn't buy you enough water to live there very long.

> [We're learning more about Mike's world. Some of these details are just that; others may pay off later if we need to take a zeppelin ride or soak a Prairie ghost town with rain.]

When the SeaBus reached Lonsdale Quay, he waited until almost everyone else was off before he went through the door. With his legs so shaky, he was afraid of falling under the crowd's feet.

The uphill walk on Lonsdale from the Quay seemed to take a long time. It was dark, and not many streetlights were working. The streetcars stopped running at 7:00, and besides he was trying to save money. The traffic was mostly pedicabs, with a few cars: gaters checking out the girls on the street corners. An armored CanSec patrol car cruised by, the first one Mike could remember seeing in weeks. The Coporation, people called them, and while CanSec wasn't as popular as the Mounties had been, it usually left people alone. Especially when they'd just been mugged, Mike thought.

> ["Gaters" are affluent Vancouverites living in gated communities. Given the cost of fuel, pedicabs are a sensible alternative to owning a vehicle.]

At least he wasn't likely to be mugged again tonight. Twenty, thirty years ago, Lower Lonsdale had been a prosperous neighborhood of high-rise condos with great views of the harbor and the city and the mountains. Now the condos had been cut up into bachelor suites for immigrants and BSers, but not many crooks lived in the neighborhood. They tended to hang out near the gates close to the bridges, where they might jack a gater's car. If you were really poor, you lived way up the mountain in Ratland, squatting in one of the old houses that had no piped water anymore. No one bothered you there because the smell was so bad.

[More exposition, and an implied promise that we'll visit both a gated community and Ratland.]

Some of the Lonsdale apartment buildings still had great views, but his, on West Keith Road, included the trucks and vans right across the street in Victoria Park. Now everyone called it "the parking lot." It wasn't very big, just a block wide and a few blocks long, but he recalled it as a nice patch of green with chestnut trees, a jogging path, and a monument to Canada's war dead. The homeless and illegals lived there now, people who didn't even qualify for BS. Most of them lived in ancient SUVs and vans and an occasional RV, mysteriously towed to the park and parked in tidy rows.

They were okay, mostly, but some of their kids could pick pockets like champions. And they'd tapped into the electricity supply to a couple of the buildings on the other side of the parking lot. So far they hadn't tried it with his building. He didn't know what he'd do if they did.

[Apart from being a social nuisance in the neighborhood, the illegals are going to be a solution for some of Mike's later problems.]

The eye-recognition lock let him into the lobby. As the building manager he could have had the big apartment on the main floor. But he'd picked a one-room studio on the fifth floor, so he could get around faster when he checked on the tenants. Most of them were old people, living on pensions that didn't go very far. The owners' agent had made it clear: don't let anyone die and rot in their apartment.

[More demographic extrapolation: This is a society of the very old.]

His studio had pretty good plumbing and no air-conditioning. When he let himself in, the heat was stupefying. Opening the sliding glass door to the balcony would only let in the smell from the parking lot's latrines. He turned on the table fan, and it began to push hot air back and forth.

A meter-square pixelite screen was sprayed on the west wall. When not in use, it was supposed to run ads, but he'd hacked them out. He'd also programmed the screen to give him a view of Vancouver in the 1600s, a million huge cedars and Douglas firs overlooking an empty inlet and a couple of villages, as seen from just this location. The only movement was the wind in the nearby trees, smoke from the village longhouses, and sometimes a canoe or an orca moving slowly across the water.

[Pixelite is a form of nanotech, essential even in a society where nanotech is suppressed. Mike's Edenic vision of pre-European Vancouver will come true at the end of the story.]

Mike slumped onto the couch and watched the light fade from the sky over ancient Burrard Inlet. Finally the screen showed only a couple of sparks, village fires on the stony beaches. The stars of 1650 came out in the black sky.

In the screen's lower right-hand corner, a row of green lights told him none of the tenants had called him while he was out. Out of habit, he ran the nightly scan: electricity consumption, water consumption, drainage check, hall cams, external cams. Everything okay. He could check the apartment bugs too, but the building's computer would have alerted him to screaming or prolonged silence, and especially to anyone calling for help. Checking without those alerts amounted to snooping. He liked his tenants. They deserved to be left alone.

[This is a kind of Orwellian telescreen, and it will come in handy on several occasions over the next few weeks. Since the building is a metaphor for Mike's own mind, the screen foreshadows his imminent access to his nonconscious selves.]

Mike shut down the scan. He knew Jer would disapprove of celebrating his diagnosis with a couple of beers. The first one went quickly, but he nursed the second one. The thought of supper crossed his mind and disappeared. Finally he tapped his arm and said to it, "Wake up."

The pixelite screen blanked, then displayed the genii. *"What is your command, O master?"*

"Give me the pancreatic cancer files and Jeremy's diagnosis again, please."

"Your wish is my command."

It scrolled up the window, complete with good 3-D graphics of the tumors. Some web graphics gave him a comparison. Yes, they looked pretty well advanced. The file contained a video of the whole interview as well; Mike thought he looked either calm or stupid when Jer broke the news.

[We are learning more about Mike's detached attitude toward himself as well as others.]

"Back to the window," he said, and again he was looking at a dark summer night in 1650, with moonlight gleaming on quiet water. The great earthquake of 1700 was still half a century ahead, and life was good.

The other lights in the apartment were off, and it was comforting to sit in the darkness, listening to the homeless in the parking lot singing and laughing. A lot of them were Mexican these days, and they loved to sing. Some guy with a great tenor was belting out some ancient pop song: *Corazón ... que ha sentido el calor de una linda mujer en las noches de octubre.* He knew enough Spanish from his years in Argentina to know what it meant. *Oh heart, which has felt the heat of a beautiful woman in the nights of October.*

He wondered if he would last until October. With his feet on the plastic coffee table, he watched the fires glowing in the vanished villages until he fell asleep.

[Mike has lived alone for several years with no sexual relationships; the song is a reminder of his solitude.]

A couple of hours later his bladder woke him up. He stumbled to the toilet, dropped his pants and sat pissing for a long time. "Radio," he said.